T0286195

No Endings, Only Beginnings

ALSO BY
BERNIE S. SIEGEL, M.D.

Books

101 Exercises for the Soul
365 Prescriptions for the Soul
The Art of Healing
A Book of Miracles
Faith, Hope & Healing
*Help Me to Heal**
How to Live Between Office Visits
Love, Animals & Miracles
Love, Magic & Mudpies
Love, Medicine & Miracles
Peace, Love & Healing
Prescriptions for Living

Children's Books

Buddy's Candle
Smudge Bunny

Audio Products

*Daily Meditations for Optimal Health**

*Healing Relationships**

*Meditations for Finding the Key to Good Health**

*Meditations for Peace of Mind**

*Meditations for Overcoming Life's Stresses and Strains**

*Finding Your True Self**

*Meditations for Morning and Evening**

*Meditations for Enhancing Your Immune System**

*Healing Meditations**

*Getting Ready**

No Endings, Only Beginnings

A DOCTOR'S NOTES ON LIVING, LOVING, AND LEARNING WHO YOU ARE

BERNIE S. SIEGEL, M.D.
with CYNTHIA J. HURN

HAY HOUSE, INC.
Carlsbad, California • New York City
London • Sydney • New Delhi

Published in the United States by: Hay House, Inc.: www.hay house.com® • ***Published in Australia by:*** Hay House Australia Pty. Ltd.: www.hayhouse.com.au • ***Published in the United Kingdom by:*** Hay House UK, Ltd.: www.hayhouse.co.uk • ***Published in India by:*** Hay House Publishers India: www.hayhouse.co.in

Cover design: The Book Designers
Interior design: Nick C. Welch

Cataloging-in-Publication Data is on file at the Library of Congress

Hardcover ISBN: 978-1-4019-58046
e-book ISBN: 978-1-4019- 58053
Audiobook ISBN: 978-1-4019- 58060

10 9 8 7 6 5 4 3 2 1
1st edition, May 2020

Printed in the United States of America

To my grandson, who taught us all to live life to the fullest and to love, laugh, and enjoy each day, no matter what challenges we face. Jason was a brave young man whose last message to us was thanking us for the loving care and protection we provided for him.

Jason Lee McGaha
August 6, 1997–August 9, 2019

CONTENTS

INTRODUCTION

Make your own Bible. Select and collect all those words and sentences that in all your reading have been to you like the blast of a trumpet.

– **Ralph Waldo Emerson** (1803–1882),
American writer and leader of the
transcendentalist movement

In January 2018, Bobbie Siegel, my soul mate and wife of 63 years, died. Over the following months, I began to sort through the copious stacks of notebooks and pieces of paper that one collects in a lifetime. I found many of the letters, interviews, notes, and sayings that had supported me in the past. Each time I read them, I was filled with wonder because they were still pertinent, still fresh and meaningful to me today. Rediscovering these valuable pieces of wisdom motivated me to write this book to share with you the mysteries and miracles of life, death, and beyond.

I agree with Emerson. Everybody should create a personal Bible—a life manual I have come to refer to as a Bible II—from such words and phrases that trumpet truth, love, and hope. After all, when you buy a new appliance, you get a service manual to help you use it properly and care for it. Why not have a manual for living, loving, healing, and growing? We can make one for ourselves by seeking wise words from those who've already sought—and found—answers to life's mysteries. Creating your own life manual gives you the opportunity to choose the sayings that speak loudest to you and that suit your unique nature. It becomes something that can grow with you over a lifetime and help you to absorb life's lessons.

We have teachers and coaches all around us. I learned, for example, that my family, colleagues, patients, medical students, and friends are all my teachers. Some of my best guideposts for living and growing were found in poetry, lectures, books, and articles. I knew the words were important when they seemed to jump off the page as if they'd been waiting for me to discover them. At other times the lyrics of a song or lines in a play felt like God was speaking directly to me, guiding me and answering my questions. I've also found that if you want to know the truth about life, you should read literary fiction. The great authors create characters who teach us wisdom through their actions, growth, and transformation. Psychoanalyst Carl Jung, playwright and storyteller

William Saroyan, and spiritual scientist Ernest Holmes are three of my favorite teachers, whose wisdom I will share using several of their quotes.

My journey of understanding has taken many paths, from science and philosophy to spirituality and literature, from relationships with family, patients, and others to communion with God, guides, and angels. All these paths have merged into my life's work. When I speak of communicating with God, I am aware that some people don't feel comfortable with the word or the concept of "God." Let me just explain that my definition of God is this: A Loving, Intelligent, and Conscious Energy. The first letters spell ALICE. Some refer to God as the Universe, Great Spirit, Allah, the Creator, or another name, but feel free, if it suits you, to just use ALICE. It doesn't matter what term you choose, as no word suffices for that which isn't nameable. The important thing to remember is that God's mind and humanity's mind are both parts of The One Mind. We need to connect to our greater consciousness—our Higher Selves—and realize it within us. Until we see it in everything and everywhere, it is difficult, if not impossible, to grasp the big picture, to understand what life is about and why we're all here. So slow down and take time to feel the presence within. Take time to read, observe, and listen.

In 1986, I wrote my first book in the hope that I could change the way people thought about health, disease, healing, and medicine. I integrated psychology, spirituality, and mysticism with practical medicine in order to help people to adopt a wholeness approach, a mind-body-spirit form of healing. Modern medical thinking at that time separated the mental, physical, and spiritual aspects of people, without any overlap. We had specialists who had no idea of you, their patient, as an integrated creation. They saw you as a mechanical entity and fixed the part that wasn't working by giving you a pill or doing a procedure versus treating the holistic issue. While things have improved in many ways, each generation still needs to learn the lessons of mind-body-spirit healing and carry them into future generations.

I have since written many books, but this time I wanted to provide people with a few thoughts from my notebooks. I have chosen to share with you quotes and phrases from a wide field of cultures, religions, and philosophy, followed by my own life stories and commentary. I cover life lessons in the practical, mystical, and spiritual realms. Practical or scientific lessons help you to survive life's difficulties, while the mystical and spiritual lessons help you to heal and to live in joy and awe. We need to integrate all three realms in order to live our healthiest, most meaningful lives and achieve our full potential.

For eight decades I have watched people deal with serious and minor problems, sometimes in very difficult and painful circumstances. Often it isn't until we reach a point of crisis in our lives that we are motivated to ask the big questions, seeking to understand life with all its mysteries, joys, and sorrows. The very act of asking opens the door to our conscious connection with God or the Universe. Once the door opens, we can choose to stay where we are or walk through to join the path of enlightenment. Even if your life is running smoothly at this time, I encourage you not to wait for a crisis. Start asking the big questions now. Now is always the right time.

I hope you will find value in the collection of quotes and stories that I have gathered here. Some I have shared in my books before, while others are new. I find that the truth is always relevant and fresh, for when you are ready for the lesson, old words will dance with new meaning and be helpful to you. The words of enlightened beings deliver the same basic message using different phraseology or stories each time. But when these things are repeated over thousands of years in many cultures and societies, it's a good sign that there is truth in the words and great value in the message. They help us through the difficult days as well as the easier times.

I wish I had had all this wisdom in my heart when Bobbie died. The grief of losing her left me drained and brokenhearted, and I went through weeks of mechanical motions, just trying to get through the day. But writing this book is restoring my love of life. It brought many moments of joy, for the awareness of Bobbie and of her loving spirit was always there, close beside me.

So please, read on. Let this be the beginning of your life manual, your own Bible II. Be inspired by poets like Emerson. Start collecting for yourself those phrases and sayings that trumpet their message straight to your heart the way the quotes in this book speak to mine. Let the words help you to find faith, grow, and heal. Rest your mind and heart in God, nature, and the Universe, knowing that you are part of the Creator and creation. Let ALICE enlighten your path as you embark upon your journey, your quest for understanding.

BEGIN YOUR QUEST FOR TRUTH

Where is God in all of this? You ask yourself, head in your hands, water washing over your body from a shower or the rain or your tears. Where is God in all of this? The question echoes across the whole of the gymnasium as your peers laugh, and the fear sets in. Where is God in all of this? It is a question we all ask at some point in our lives. . . . Turn the question inward and let it reverberate through your heart, your mind, your soul, every fiber of your very being. Where is God in all of this? He is in your heart, in your breath; He is in every action you take and in every life you touch. Will you accept His presence here? Will you act as an agent of miracles today? Where is God in all of this? God is with me and I am with God. Repeat it, feel it, live it.

– **Charlie Siegel**,
Excerpted from his unpublished poem,
"*The Answer Lies Within*"

This poem was written by our grandson, a young adult who amazes me with his beautiful thoughts and words. Charlie understands that you have to ask the difficult questions in order to grow in wisdom, faith, and strength. Creative writing is just one of the paths he takes to enter the classroom of the soul. Like so many others, he's found that the big questions always involve God and the meaning of life. Why are we here? What is the truth?

What many people don't realize is that life, of itself, has no meaning. Life is simply a mechanical event, an expression of God's existence and curiosity. Being in the body presents us with opportunities to creatively act out the Creator's desire and intention to experience, learn, and love. We discover through our individual experiences what makes our lives meaningful and where God is in all of it.

How we use our minds and bodies—and whether we contribute to or become destructive to the process of life—determines whether we grow. Meaning arises when we make mindful choices from what is placed before us: life and death, good and evil, and so on. The meaning our lives take on relates to those choices and who or what we see as our "Lord" or our path. We can live a life based upon greed, power, and selfish desires, seeking out material things, or a life based on bringing truth and love into the world.

As humans we get to choose our Lord—our path. If that choice takes us into darkness and misery, we can always alter our choice and live in light and love. As Charlie's poem says, our God is revealed in our hearts, our breath, our actions, and in every person whose life we touch.

If you believe that you only affect the people and things immediately around you, your thinking is too small. In order to grow in wisdom, you need to expand your view. No matter what choices we make, we are the extension of God's arms, the expression of God's desire to learn and expand. Everything we say, think, and do becomes part of everything. When we choose a path of truth and love, we can even become agents of miracles.

Think of all the stars whose light travels forever through the darkest reaches of space, even after they burn out. When the light of one star causes wonder in the heart and mind of a human, that star becomes meaningful. When clouds or daylight block the view, the connection between man and star is still just as real. The effect of our life upon the universe is no different; the connections between us, God, and all creation are happening all the time, whether we see them or not.

Charlie inspires me, not just because of his quest for truth, but also because he makes a mantra to live by: "God is with me and I am with God." When we choose such thoughts as these, we are never alone. We enter a classroom for the soul with curiosity and faith, and life becomes an experience of wonder and awe. I encourage you now to sit quietly for a moment and think about your own quest for truth. God is sitting right beside you, so what questions will you ask? What answers do you seek from the Universe?

Ask Yourself Who You Are

Remember that you are an actor in a play, and the Playwright chooses the manner of it: if he wants it short, it is short; if long, it is long. If he wants you to act a poor man you must act the part with all your powers; and so if your part be a cripple or a magistrate or a plain man. For your business is to act the character that is given you and act it well; the choice of the cast is Another's.

– **Epictetus** (55–135),
Roman slave and Greek philosopher

Epictetus, born into Roman slavery in the country now named Turkey, embraced life with all he had. We can learn much from him, for despite lameness and ill health, he educated himself by listening to great philosophers and teachers. His intelligence and wisdom played a large part in his release from slavery, and he went on to become a great teacher. Epictetus said that the only things he truly owned were his will and his purpose. He accepted that his imperfect body and difficult life circumstances were necessary to achieve his soul's desire for growth. They were perfect gifts from God. It was up to him to make the gifts meaningful.

Entering the physical body is like leaving your spiritual home and going to school, moving up through the grades and helping your classmates until commencement day. Our job is to do our best with what we have, whether we live 9 minutes or 90 years. The grace of God always accompanies us as we enter the body, for we are to expand that grace and pass it on to others through our love and endeavors, contributing and co-creating in our own manner.

You might wonder, *But what about babies or children who die? How can they contribute or co-create?* I promise you that even a newborn who dies at birth serves his or her parents. Experiencing the loss of their baby teaches parents many lessons about loving, letting go, and turning grief into something meaningful. For others who are physically afflicted or who endure any form of restricted life circumstances, there are always opportunities for learning and sharing their gifts. Sometimes just being—the fact of their existence—is the gift.

I once met a young woman who was born without arms and hands. She adopted the attitude of Epictetus and lived her life with passion. She rode horses in national competitions and fed herself by holding a fork with her bare feet. It amazed me because she never asked for pity or said, "I'm not like other people and never will be." She was an inspiration for everyone who met her.

Think of the ugly duckling story; no matter how hard he tried, he could not be like the other ducks. It wasn't until he looked into the still pond and asked "Who am I?" that the reflection of his true self revealed he was a beautiful swan. All of us—no matter what we look like or what our situation is—are perfect, beautiful souls embarking on a human journey.

The wisdom of Epictetus is as relevant today as it was 2,000 years ago. We all need to play our assigned character as best we can and contribute what we can. We all need to dig deep in order to recognize our real purpose and give it all we've got. The fact that you are here means your spirit is ready to grow. Go ahead and ask yourself now, "Who am I?" Then sit quietly and listen as your question reaches out. Open your mind to the possibility that you are a co-creator, that you are God-in-training.

Seek the Reason for Suffering and Pain

There is no such thing as learning to be whole without being tested. Staggering about in pain or bewilderment, we are learning the choice: to be bitter . . . or to surrender to love.

– **Clarissa Pinkola Estés**,
PSYCHOANALYST, POET, AND AUTHOR OF
Women Who Run with the Wolves

Estés is a cantadora—a keeper of the old stories—who teaches wisdom in the way of traditional storytellers. She brings up an important point about suffering: we always have a choice. Each of us must realize that yes, we will suffer in life, but the way we regard our suffering—and the choices we make in response—determines whether our trials become a curse or a blessing. If we were provided with a perfect world, there would be no purpose to our journey through life. An all-knowing, all-powerful deity must step aside, let us experience all the feelings and learn all the lessons, or life would be nothing more than a magic trick.

It is one thing to know *we* must face difficulties in life, but when a parent knows his or her child is going to suffer, it's hard to accept. We ask God, "Why my child?" And we beg, "Give me the suffering instead." Yet all we can do is love them, prepare them, and cushion their experience to make it less daunting. Even those efforts may not mitigate everything they undergo. When our son Keith needed an operation, I explained to him what happens in a hernia repair. I showed him pictures of the operating room and went into great detail about what the hospital was like, the people he would meet, and so forth. When the day came, he did fine until he awakened in the recovery room. He looked up at me with big sad eyes and said, "You forgot to tell me it was going to hurt."

As a doctor I saw a lot of suffering. I couldn't understand at first why God would let these things happen, especially when the patient was a child. I had entered the field of medicine because I wanted to help people; I wanted to fix their brokenness and disease. When I couldn't cure them or ease the suffering of their families, I suffered too. Emotional pain, sorrow, frustration, and even anger rose out of my powerlessness to fix everything. These uncomfortable feelings became the catalyst for my own inner search. My pain, my suffering stirred up the soil of my soul, and the question *Why do they suffer?* became the seed of my awakening.

One time, when I asked God why he had made a world full of disease, war, cruelty, and all kinds of difficulties between people and nations, he answered me in a dream. He took me to the Garden of Eden. It was a modern-day Eden with cars and traffic signals, but all the traffic was backed up.

Half of the people were saying, "I love you. You go first."

The other half were replying, "No, you go first; I love you." Everybody was acting loving toward everybody else, and no one was going anywhere. It quickly became obvious what kinds of problems a perfect world would pose, and I got the point.

As for the question *Why pain?* the biological reason for pain—whether emotional or physical—is that it protects you, directs you, and helps you to grow and change. All of our choices relate to pain. Freedom from pain may seem idyllic, but I must warn you, we need it to survive. Not having physical pain to alert us is dangerous; we would lose parts of our bodies from injury or infection, and diseases would go undiagnosed until too late.

Humans were designed so that we *decide* what to do with our pain. If you pick up a burning object that is too hot to hold, you can drop it to protect your hand, or you can override that decision and carry the burning object out of the house to save your home and family. An automatic stimulus reaches your brain, but you create the response. Your response is not a reflex but a chosen reaction, incredible in its rapidity and appropriateness. Considering how complex some split-second decisions are, it seems miraculous.

Emotional pain becomes a labor pain of self-birth or, if ignored, is wasted in needless suffering. Giving birth to yourself is the issue—after you do, you will be amazed at how your pain diminishes and heals. One person who understood this, and who never chose to be bitter about her challenges, was Helen Keller. Despite being born healthy, she was stricken profoundly deaf and blind after a childhood fever. Keller actually described her suffering as being the pain from which "the violets of patience and sweetness" grow. She learned that suffering opens the door to a deeper knowledge and emotional awareness. In many cases, it also motivates us to give ourselves permission to live differently and transform ourselves. I often think of coal: when it is compressed for long enough, the coal molecules crystalize and turn into diamonds.

Do life's difficulties and our suffering mean that we did something wrong or we're being punished? No! That is just life. Even death is necessary for life. Pain and suffering are gifts that few people want or understand, but the person who accepts these gifts helps us all. I can't emphasize too strongly how necessary they are for a healthy life.

Some of the choices we make in order to avoid pain are self-destructive and close the door of communication with God. Distractions, emotional numbness, addictions, and avoidance are common examples. Those who are willing to go into the darkness of their souls and confront the cause of the pain will change in a way that helps them. Remember, when you hit bottom, it is painful, but by hitting the bottom, you stir up the earth, and that makes the best sowing ground for new life and growth. Sometimes we need an elevator to help us climb out of our pit. When you need a quick lift, let others point out where the elevator is located. Realize, too, that you can also be helped by the elevator operator *and* its occupants. Twelve-step programs are an excellent example. Guidance doesn't have to come directly from God; it often comes from your interaction with people.

Don't be afraid to move forward. Live in the knowledge that you are never alone. Be open to guidance and growth so that you can hear God's voice in its many forms. Remember, the word *guidance* is made up of "God, you, and I dance." What I ask of you is to not bury God's voice when you are in pain and to not become bitter when you suffer. Instead, hold your pain in this moment of consciousness. Breathe it in, and let your questions rise to your lips. Go ahead and ask, "What is the lesson, God? What am I here to learn?" Then surrender to the lesson. Surrender, indeed, to love.

Explore Your Faith

We are surrounded by an Infinite Possibility. It is Goodness, Life, Law and Reason. In expressing Itself through us, It becomes more fully conscious of Its own being. Therefore, It wishes to express through us. . . . It can pass into expression through us only as we consciously allow It to do so. Therefore, we should have faith in It, and Its desires and Its ability to do for us all that we should ever need to have done. *Since It must pass through our consciousness to operate for us, we must be conscious that It is doing so.*

– **Ernest Holmes** (1887–1960),
American founder of the Religious Science Movement and author of *The Science of Mind*

Holmes uses the term *Infinite Possibility* in the way we might use *God* or *the path*. The possibility is what God hopes for us, and the infinite is what we are, will become, and keep becoming. We must consciously seek to be reflections of our Higher Selves and have faith that our Creator will provide everything we need for this to happen.

Faith is usually defined in two basic ways, the first a strong religious belief based on the fear of what will happen to unbelievers and the second a strong belief based on trust and confidence. The word *confidence* means "with faith." In either case, faith is a choice—a decision. It doesn't just happen. What Holmes is telling us is that a conscious commitment to God-in-us is necessary to our very being if we wish to tap into God's grace—the loving, intelligent, conscious energy that does for us all we ever need to have done.

If you shut the door of your conscious mind because you can't see "It," you might never hear God whispering outside that door. To experience faith, you need to remain willing to listen with your inner self and keep the door open, even when nothing appears to you at that moment. If some miraculous or mystical thing happens, accept your experience; don't discount it just because you can't explain it. If you want explanations or proof before you believe what happened, you risk closing the door.

When you enter a state of faith, the love and awe of God follows—you begin to reside in the realm of "Goodness, Life, Law, and Reason." You no longer believe you are alone, for you experience the connection to something greater than yourself. Having faith doesn't mean we won't have difficulties or problems—that's life. And having problems does not mean your faith was placed in the wrong thing or that your prayers weren't answered. The Oneness—the voice—is there to support and sustain us throughout those difficulties while we learn how to deal with them and utilize them in a meaningful way. When you have faith and something goes wrong, you no longer ask, "Why me?" You say, "Please give me the strength and show me the way. Teach me what I need to know."

Perhaps the most powerful prayer for strengthening your faith is the one that just says "Thank you." Gratitude expresses confidence in the greater good. When we recognize that our trials are gifts, we open the door wide so the lessons can pour in. We don't brace our bodies against the door and set an attitude of resistance, hoping to stem the tide—we welcome the lesson to come in a great or small wave. And however it comes, we begin by learning to ride that wave as best we can. Many gifts—such as comfort, peace, humility, and compassion—also come pouring through the open door. We never achieve perfection, but willingness to learn helps us to live in faith and grow in the conscious awareness of God-in-us.

When I was young, any time things didn't happen the way I wanted, my mother, whose faith was as real and solid as anything you can touch, would say, "God is redirecting you. Something good will come of this." And she was right.

One example happened when I was nearing the end of high school and I applied to Harvard. Why Harvard? I was a very bright kid, but I didn't have any specific reason or desire to go there, except that it would look good and sound good on my record.

The guidance counselor and the principal of my high school felt a smaller university would better suit my personality and needs. My principal, a graduate of Colgate, wanted me to attend his alma mater. Finally the day came when I got the letter from Harvard. They didn't accept me. So I asked myself, *Now what do you do? You can go to your room crushed, or you can say, "I am not supposed to go to Harvard."* I remembered my mother's words and chose to have faith that God was redirecting me. Sure enough, a few weeks later, God sent a letter saying, "Go to Colgate." God was right again, and so was my principal. I went. I also won competitive scholarships for New York State residents who were attending college in the state. I wouldn't have qualified for the scholarships if I'd gone to Harvard, and winning them removed my sense of guilt about putting such a big financial strain on my dad.

Colgate worked out beautifully for me. I don't think I would have been as well-off at Harvard—a large school in a big city. Instead, I was at a small, not co-ed (at that time) school in upstate New York, where my personality, skills, and abilities fit in. The better choice was the feeling choice, not the intellectual one. Having faith in a loving intelligence and the idea that God was redirecting me threw the window of "Infinite Possibilities" wide open.

A great example of how faith works is illustrated by a news article I once read about a blind man who had just walked the entire Appalachian Trail. His comment was that he couldn't see the Appalachian Trail; he just took it. Think about that. He knew the trail was there for him to take. He could "see" through the darkness of his blindness. That's what faith is—you just do it, and everything else falls into place.

My hope is that this deeper knowledge will come to you—this intuitive quality that knows the way, doesn't need a map, and doesn't need to see. The map is in you because the vision is in you and the voice directs you. All you have to do is set your course and go. Faith knows the best path to take. Experience the journey and absorb the lessons your Higher Self desires for you. As Holmes suggested, you must *consciously* allow the Infinite Possibility to "pass into expression" through you. Go ahead; embark on your journey now—walk the path of Goodness, Life, Law, and Reason.

WHICH WAY

What should I do when I have a choice?
Which fork in the road do I follow?
Follow the right fork by taking them both
They are the beginning of a circle you cannot see
All roads lead to the same place
They bring you home like a river that flows to the sea
They bring you home, completing the circle of life

2

LIVE AUTHENTICALLY

We are more than a body and a brain: we are also a soul and spirit. But humans are forgetful animals. We forget that we have a story beyond our current circumstances, that we may have come into this world with an assignment and an identity that predate our present lives and won't end when our present bodies are left behind. Forgetting who we are, and what our soul's purpose is in this world, we get into all kinds of trouble.

– **Robert Moss**,
Australian author and creator of Active Dreaming Workshops

When we live authentic lives, we are fulfilling the desires of our souls. As Moss teaches, when we lose track of our dreams and soul urgings, we begin to feel separated from that inner voice, that conscious connection with our Higher Selves. The only way to regain our sense of connection is to revisit our dreams, reveal our deepest feelings, and identify once again with the urgings of our souls. This brings about a total state of integration and wellness.

Children are born authentic, but over time parents, teachers, and other authority figures shape them and prod them to chase goals that are aligned with family expectations, social values, and religious beliefs. Provided they feel loved and receive the right messages, this is a good thing, but there comes a day when all children, regardless of their circumstances, are old enough to make their own choices. If the choices we make are not in balance with our true natures—in alignment with our souls' desires—we lose our authentic selves.

Not living authentically subjects your body, mind, and emotions to unnecessary stress because you abandon your true nature. I know many people who died of serious illnesses from spending their lives trying to fulfill their parents' dream, while those who realized their error—quit their financially imposed job, made life changes, and embraced their authentic selves—experienced a fraction of the illnesses and lived longer, happier lives.

Getting to know the real you takes courage. As Robert Moss points out, sometimes people lose their real selves after a traumatic event. For many who experience trauma, it becomes easier to hide behind a role or a mask than to be vulnerable and express their real feelings with humility, honesty, and self-compassion. A good example would be soldiers who are deployed into battle zones or police and ambulance drivers who suffer secondary trauma from what they witness. If they develop an iron mask of heroism and never express their fear or sense of horror, their old personalities get buried and disappear. Trauma will change you, but you can learn how to let those changes be transformational and beautiful.

If you wish to know yourself and live an authentic life, you need to accept your inadequacies, fears, weaknesses, mistakes, and more. You also need to identify what makes you come alive with enthusiasm, curiosity, and wonder. Only then can you make the changes that serve you. But how do we go about finding our true selves? There are many ways to reestablish the connection with your soul. Moss, for example, runs workshops using a combination of lucid dreaming and shamanism. Some people go for counseling or do various forms of meditation, mindfulness, body work, and other creative therapies.

How does one know when they are living an authentic life? If you're not certain whether you are, spend some time totally alone in quiet stillness, without electronic devices or other distractions, and see how you feel. Constant distractions and noise stop us from being alone with our thoughts and feelings. If you are comfortable with an hour of stillness, then I would say you are in the process of knowing yourself. Knowing yourself means being willing to be with yourself. Once you can do that, the frantic search for distraction and escape will stop ruling your life, and you can choose to fill your life with the things that bring you joy. I have spent a lifetime learning to live authentically and to know who I am. I was amazed at how well I have done since my wife died and I had to face living alone for the very first time. I do miss her terribly, but I am okay being with myself because I live my truth.

If you feel discomfort at being alone, or you are unhappy with any aspect of your life, read on. Use this section as a prompt to find the person you forgot. Seek quotes and affirmations that support you and give you permission to be yourself. Put them in your Bible II. Get ready to be reunited with the urgings of your soul. Your authentic life is waiting.

Practice Emotional Honesty

[To attempt] to be "normal" is a splendid ideal for the unsuccessful, for all those who have not yet found an adaptation. But for people who have far more ability than the average, for whom it was never hard to gain successes and to accomplish their share of the world's work—for them restriction to the normal signifies . . . unbearable boredom, infernal sterility and hopelessness. As a consequence there are as many people who become neurotic because they are only normal, as there are people who are neurotic because they cannot become normal.

– **CARL GUSTAV JUNG** (1875–1961),
SWISS PSYCHIATRIST AND FOUNDER OF
ANALYTICAL PSYCHIATRY

Fitting in with your family's or society's idea of "normal" causes more problems than people realize. Jung—a wise and kind healer of the psyche—saw, in his practice, many people driven to neuroses of various kinds. In my practice as a surgeon and doctor, I saw many people driven to cancer, other diseases, and death. I like to warn people that "fake it till you make it," a frequently heard piece of advice, should come with a caution sticker. Too much faking can literally ruin your life.

As we try to be "normal" day after day, year after year, we become used to pretending. Our habit of fitting in with the status quo and pleasing others makes us blind to the many times that our behavior goes in one direction while our true feelings are going in the other, thus creating inner conflict or dissociation. This habit is called *emotional dishonesty,* and it is something we *all* learn to do. The repercussions of such self-denial over many years can be anything from mild to severe and can cause physical disease and mental illness, which affect the whole family.

Denial of our true feelings and continually putting our needs aside in order to please others are two of the most common forms of emotional dishonesty. Sometimes our work or family responsibilities make total self-sacrifice seem inevitable, but that isn't healthy. What we need to do in such cases is to set aside a regular time—actually set up a recurring, unbreakable appointment for ourselves—and use this time to do some activity that replenishes us and allows some form of creative expression. You shouldn't feel guilty for taking time off or spending a longer-than-usual time away. Don't become sick from doing things that you do for love. Be healthy and vibrant from doing the things that you do *just for the love of doing them.*

Doctors and nurses are masters of emotional dishonesty. They are always caring for others and rarely spend time caring for themselves. After I completed medical school and my practice as a surgeon progressed, I felt the chronic pain of being a physician, and each year it grew more and more acute. By pain I mean seeing the human difficulties and making hard decisions—not being able to cure everyone, not preventing every disease, seeing complications arise from medical care, or watching children you care about die and knowing you can't stop it.

Physicians are not trained properly in how to deal with their emotional pain. We were told that we must adopt a stance of detached concern to protect ourselves. How can you have *detached* concern? That term alone is an oxymoron. It really means you detach from your heart, your real self. What doctors need to learn is *compassionate caring.* For years I had been hiding my feelings behind the surgeon's mask. I would be saying to patients, "I need to hug you," thinking I was giving them compassionate caring. I finally woke up to the fact that it started with *I need,* and I began to apologize for turning my patients into my therapists. They all responded, "We knew you needed it. So we hugged you." I learned that I have to take care of Bernie too.

People-pleasing is a common example of emotional dishonesty in the form of self-denial. If your mind says no to someone's request but your mouth says yes, it's time to look at that. If it seems easier to say "Okay, I'll come to your dinner party" rather than risk hurting the host's feelings, understand that you deny *your* true feelings if you accept—you are being dishonest with yourself.

I am sure that Jung would join me in advising you that it is *okay* and far better to just say no. The word *no* is a complete sentence. If you can't manage a no, try saying, "I'll think about it and get back to you later." After gathering your thoughts, you can call them back and say, "I won't be going, but thank you for asking me." You don't need to give an excuse. If you're afraid you'll say the wrong thing, take the advice given by Lily Tomlin to a violinist when he stopped her to ask, "How do I get to Carnegie Hall?" She answered, "Practice, practice, practice." I encourage you to do the same. Stand in front of a mirror and practice your response: "No." "Thank you, but no." "Hell no!" and so on. Note: it is okay to laugh at yourself.

Living the life that others choose for you and trying to achieve their idea of normal is not why God gave us freedom of choice. Common symptoms of someone practicing emotional dishonesty are self-medicating or addictive behaviors. These choices numb the urgings of the hungry soul. Other emotionally dishonest people become workaholics to avoid facing the empty vessel of their ignored lives. Constantly focusing on other people's problems is another sign of living without authenticity. These people may be denying an unhealed trauma from the past or refusing to accept that something in their current lives isn't working for them. It is important to understand that *you cannot heal what you do not feel,* and you cannot fix that which you hide from. To live an authentic life, you must be in touch with your feelings and follow your heart. You must learn to be emotionally honest with others and not deny yourself so much of the time. You must also learn to ask for help and accept help when it is offered to you. Don't abandon yourself.

Finally, there are those who have a dream that dances like a flame in their heart, but they are afraid of failure. They hem and they haw. They focus on every obstacle and listen to people who say their ideas are crazy—they're never going to happen. Every time they do this, the inner flame flickers, until one day, it finally goes out. Second-guessing yourself and believing you aren't good enough, or fearing that you might fail, is questioning God's ability to use you as His tool. Who are you not to use what you were uniquely given? Who are you not to follow your dream? God planted that seed; it is up to you to water and nourish it.

If you have a dream and you want to do or be something else, take a step today toward your goal. It doesn't matter whether that means paging through that college brochure, signing up for that scuba diving class, or starting your own knitting blog. Just keep taking one step forward every day. When obstacles appear, look for a route around them and ask for help when needed. Yes, you may be taking a risk, and you may fail. But you can always try again, this time a little smarter. Not listening to your soul's desire is a form of death.

Be emotionally honest with yourself. Did you stifle a childhood passion to grow up and become an astronaut? It may be that you'll never go on a space mission, but there are other ways you can experience, express, and share your love for space and for the science of getting there. Seek that other way. Don't adopt a neurosis just to survive. Whatever your passion is, follow it. Go ahead—make your own normal and see just how amazing that is.

Respect the Power of Words

Words saturated with sincerity, conviction, faith, and intuition are like highly explosive vibration bombs, which, when set off, shatter the rocks of difficulties and create the change desired.

– **PARAMAHANSA YOGANANDA** (1893–1952),
INDIAN YOGI AND MEDITATION GURU

Words, as Yogananda teaches, have incredible energy. He encouraged people to use affirmations: positive statements repeated daily that help you to challenge negative beliefs about yourself, overcome pessimistic thinking, and eliminate self-sabotaging behaviors. Louise Hay turned her life around using such affirmations and saved the lives of many others when she brought the practice into popular use.

Wordplay is also a powerful tool for embracing life's lessons. Yes, you *can* play with words, as my children showed me. My son Jeff had a license plate made that read, EVIL. When I asked why he wanted that on his car, he replied, "People look in their rear-view mirror, and EVIL becomes LIVE." I often speak about the drawing another son brought home from school with "words" written many times over in a connected pattern. "Wordswordswords" began to look like "swordswordswords." The message of his drawing was that words not only bring us together but can also tear us apart. I was amazed that a child could have such wisdom.

A lack of the right words in our lives can even kill us. As we are told by the sages, the power of life and death resides in the tongue, and while many have fallen by the edge of the sword, many more have been injured by the sharpened tongue. Social media has highlighted this truth. Today, kids are taking their own lives over things said to them or written about them on the Internet. At the same time, others are saved from the brink when words of kindness, comfort, and support give them the acceptance they need.

Your body instinctively understands the energy of words. You can benefit from this inner knowledge by paying attention to words that describe the *feeling* of your physical symptoms. Always ask yourself if the word you use to describe your symptom also describes another aspect of your life. "Aching, stiff joints" may reflect an inflexible work schedule or relationship, while a headache that feels like "constant pressure" may describe your current financial situation. In such cases, your body is begging you to take notice of what's happening in your life. Just recognizing that the symptom applies not only to your body but also to your life shatters your ability to ignore the unhealthy situation and motivates you to make the changes you need.

Sometimes a childhood tragedy or trauma affects our adult health in a negative way. Once again, the power of words can help to heal this wound. A good exercise is to write a short story about that memory, but this time, let the ending be different. Allow your intuition to lead where the story needs to go. If you feel inclined, let it be an ideal ending, the one you wish had happened. Put your heart into it. Create a new possibility. You'll be surprised at what you learn about yourself and the lessons of that trauma. When we write with "sincerity, conviction, faith, and intuition," we give ourselves a chance to heal the past and live a new life.

I often suggest that people write poetry. I'm not talking about classical or rhyming poems, necessarily, but free verse that just flows out of you, with no self-judgment on grammar, punctuation, and so on. When you give yourself permission to release words on the page in a stream-of-consciousness form, you create those "bombs" that shatter the walls around feelings you've denied. Write whatever the voice inside you says. Understand that when you write freestyle, you are listening at a deeper level to what you might never hear otherwise. It is like putting on a celestial hearing aid that amplifies the divine recording, not just the meaningless sounds and distractions of life.

Keeping a journal can be your life's poetry too. It acts as an observer who hears you better than the surrounding people, those who are not tuned in to your experience—they are unaware, not listening, or distracted. Journaling unearths your authentic self and puts you in touch with your pain.

One night, many years ago, I forgot to hide my journal. Bobbie read it and said, "There's nothing funny in this." I told her my life wasn't funny, and then she reminded me of the stories that I brought home to her and the kids about humorous things that happened at the hospital. I hadn't included them. From then on, the funny events became part of my journal too. By writing lighthearted poetry and stories from a childlike view of the world, inspired by a love of what surrounds you, you can heal your life. Laughter is far more therapeutic than drugs or alcohol, and it erases all your negative feelings. It restores you. You cease being numb and begin to feel again. Fear and laughter cannot exist simultaneously, so when you write funny stories and observations, you are living in a place of acceptance and self-love.

I will share with you one of my poems, written when Bobbie was deciding whether to come with me on a tour of speaking engagements. She asked my opinion, and my honest answer inspired this entry in my journal:

A BEAUTIFUL BURDEN

"If you don't go I'll have a heavy heart
If you do go I'll have a hernia"
My wife and I often travel together
We are a team, sharing fair and foul weather
At times our travel takes us into the air
And all the luggage is in my care
Bobbie's bags would burst if packed any tighter
But I brave the chance of a hernia
For I've heard love makes one's burdens lighter
And I've learned from traveling on my own
That a lonely heart weighs much more than a bag
That can't be packed any tighter

I encourage you to start writing today. Don't say "I'm not a poet" or "I'm not creative enough." This is about your life, not whether your poems rhyme or your story pleases others. This is about you listening to the life inside you, healing you as God would—from the inside out. Take up your pen now. Sit quietly and listen for the Creator's voice from within. As you write your own reality into existence, feel the energy of those "highly explosive vibration bombs," and let your own big bang begin!

Draw Your Inner Self Out

As the poets and painters of centuries have tried to tell us, art is not about the expression of talent or the making of pretty things. It is about the preservation and containment of soul. It is about arresting life and making it available for contemplation. Art captures the eternal in the everyday, and it is the eternal that feeds soul—the whole world in a grain of sand.

– **Thomas Moore**,
American Catholic monk, psychotherapist,
and author of *Care of the Soul*

Moore, a former monk and a lover of Jung's work, delved deeply into the core of himself and his religion before finding his true purpose. I love his description of the soul because it relates to me and the many pathways I took in order to understand God, creation, and myself.

People think of me as a doctor, healer, or spiritual leader, but I am also an artist. We are all a mixture of many things, and these different roles are meant to help us to adapt and survive life's challenges. Whenever I was unhappy and feeling stressed as a physician, I would tap into the artist in me to find my sanity again. While painting, my soul was soothed, and the unhappiness and pain were transformed. Time didn't exist any longer. The art became my medicine, and I was able to continue functioning in my life.

I painted all the members of my family doing the things they loved and that reflected their true characters. The artistic results were like visual poetry—very much alive—and doing them satisfied my need to create. But when I began painting a self-portrait and looked at myself in the mirror, I saw only a masked man. Facing my feelings at that time was too difficult because it meant I had to get honest and see all my vulnerabilities. Instead, I painted my reflection wearing full surgical garb—covered and hidden from the world. No mirror could penetrate the surgeon's mask, cap, and gown to touch my real feelings. The painting I created this time did nothing to relieve my stress or soothe the discomfort of my soul. By focusing on the outer profession, I had denied my true individuality. What I didn't know then was that healing can only occur when you see and acknowledge your truth, not cover it up with a masked image. It wasn't until I joined a different kind of art class—taught by psychiatrist Elisabeth Kübler-Ross, of all people—that my inner self was uncovered in the artwork.

I'm always amazed at how effective art and visual symbols can be for helping people to get in touch with their lives and souls. When I'm giving a lecture, I will hold up a white piece of paper with a black dot on it. I ask the audience to describe what I am holding. People spend a lot of time discussing the black spot's shape, size, and dimensions, and they will go on and on, forgetting there is a big white space around it. I then tell the audience that this piece of paper represents everyone's lives, and I guide them to remember there is a great deal to life, not just the dark spots. I tell them about one woman who said, after her husband developed cancer, "Life isn't just black on white anymore—there are rainbows."

Black is made up of all the colors, and something beautiful can come out of it. We all have our difficulties—our black spots—and we all have the ability to draw out the colors of the rainbow from those spots. Think about your difficulties with that imagery in mind. What are your rainbows?

Imagine going to your surgeon for a first consultation, and before he sees you, you're asked to draw a picture with crayons and paper. You're probably thinking, "This is crazy." But art is such an intuitive window into the life and body of the artist, I used it regularly as one of my doctor's tools. In my book *The Art of Healing*, I gave instructions on how to do drawings that help to unveil your subconscious and allow it to have open communication with your conscious self. You might say it is a way of tapping into the individual eccentricity of your soul. I would tell my patients, "If your first reaction is that you are not an artist, stop worrying about failing or doing it wrong. Children love to draw and don't judge their creations harshly. Just allow your inner child to come out and play. This is not an art assignment—it is an act of love, of meeting your true self."

Why don't you try it now? Obtain plain white paper and a box of crayons or coloring pens, including black, white, brown, and all the colors of the rainbow. Holding the page in a vertical position, draw yourself. If you have a disease, take another piece of paper and draw yourself, your illness, your treatment, and your immune system eliminating the illness. Notice I said eliminate, not kill. If you have an autoimmune disease, draw your immune system behaving itself. You don't have to be fighting or killing to get well. You can heal and cure with love and nonaggressive images, such as a tumor represented by a melting ice cube.

If you would like some insight about your family struggles or work, draw yourself with your family or a picture of you at your job. You can use an outdoor scene or any background you like. When you finish your drawing, put it aside for a day or two. Then come back and look at it with someone you trust.

Even if you aren't a therapist, things in the picture can help you to see what you are holding inside.

Notice what is not in the picture, such as body parts, and what those represent. A person at work without visible hands, for example, might signify that this person can't get a handle on the job. Observe what colors you used. Are they vibrant and varied? Or is there a predominance of one color? Pay attention to where people are located in the family picture, how big the spaces are between them, and where their feet are pointing.

If you are facing treatment for cancer and you're subconsciously thinking of the chemotherapy drugs as a kind of poison with terrible side effects, your drawing will reveal those fears. One example is a patient who drew the skull and crossbones symbol on the chemotherapy bag in his picture. When someone's drawing shows such a negative image, it may mean this person needs to consider an alternative treatment, change doctors, or change his or her view of the treatment before taking the therapy. To adjust your attitude about the treatment into something that helps you heal, visualize a successful outcome 5 times a day for 10 days before you go for the first treatment. Turn the "poison" image of your initial drawing into sparkling angels of love that will enter your bloodstream and make you well.

This helps you to literally reprogram yourself. You will experience fewer or no side effects, and you will achieve a more successful outlook.

Getting your children to draw their home and family will also give you helpful insight into their feelings and the dynamics of your family interactions. When problems arise or new choices appear in your life, do another drawing: which career to follow, where to live, etc. Draw yourself in each career or in the places you're considering moving to. Your unconscious will direct you, just as it does in your dreams; all the information you need to make the right choice will be there in your drawing. I still do these drawings, and I continue to learn about myself from what ends up on the page, for I am still changing, and I love what is revealed each time.

The drawing exercise sounds simple—and it is—but the interpretation is not. You are the authority regarding your drawing, but it helps to share it with your doctor, therapist, or counselor. If you're interested in learning all the details of this technique, read my book *The Art of Healing,* Gregg Furth's *The Secret World of Drawings,* or Susan Bach's *Life Paints Its Own Span.* The drawings empower you to have faith in your decisions or to change your reality and outcome, provided you are willing to work and act as if you are the person you want to be.

I encourage you to get some crayons and make "loving art" for yourself now. You may find that expressing what you can't say in any other way—with colors, details, and shapes—reveals the eccentric, loving madness of your soul and the truth you had no words for.

3

BE AN AGENT OF CHANGE

In archery we have something like the way of the superior man. When the archer misses the centre of the target, he turns round and seeks for the cause of his failure in himself.

– **Confucius** (551–479 B.C.),
Chinese philosopher

When the master archer misses the bulls-eye, he knows there is no point in blaming the bow, the arrow, or the target. He also knows not to be harsh with himself. Missing the mark merely alerts him to set things right in his mind, focus on the moment, and regain his inner balance.

Top athletes are familiar with the principle that we create what we think. One example is the golfer: when he approaches a water hazard, if he imagines—even for a few seconds—the ball dropping into the stream, his thought is likely to produce the exact result he didn't want. But if he visualizes the ball reaching its goal, chances are much higher that the ball will sail straight over the hazard.

We are unfocused because our lives are so busy and we forget to stop, feel, and listen to our bodies. Instead we fill our minds with what ifs, should haves, must dos, and replayed arguments. We are unaware of—or we ignore—physical and emotional symptoms that act as red flags. Whenever we suffer depression, panic attacks, or physical illness, our bodies are shouting at us: "Pay attention! Your aim is off center!" They are telling us we need to focus on rebalancing our lives.

All too often, people refuse to accept any responsibility for their problems or situation. They feel victimized by someone or something, and they feel powerless over their future. But we do have choices, and while we cannot fix everything, we can certainly make things better or walk away from the cause of the problem.

Many times we honestly don't know what is wrong or how to change the circumstances that are hurting us, but there's always help available if only we ask. Some think that seeking help is a sign of weakness or selfishness. The fear of being seen as somehow faulty or "less than" might lead them to seek unhealthy coping strategies. One example is the children who turn to self-harm or drugs instead of reporting they are being bullied. They don't want their parents to know how bad they feel, or they secretly fear there really is something about them that deserves the scorn of others. What these kids don't realize is they are not alone. They think they are the only ones going through this, so they don't talk about it. We need to teach children to eliminate *what is hurting them*—not eliminate themselves. Unhealthy coping strategies, like self-harming and self-medicating, can stay with kids into their adult years. These behaviors lead to worse problems that can eventually result in serious illness and death.

Parents also need to learn how to show their children that they are loved and *worth loving*. If parenting classes became part of the standard high school and college curriculum, most of us would benefit. One long-term study of Harvard students revealed that children who grow up without feeling parental love and acceptance have a 98 percent incidence of serious illness by the time they reach middle age, four times higher than the incidence in children who felt loved and accepted. Receiving poor parenting does not need to negatively affect the rest of their lives. These students could have better results if they learn to re-parent themselves.

I remember one woman who came into my office asking for surgery. When I looked at her record, it blew me away because every few months she was undergoing surgery, some of them significant procedures. She was driving doctors crazy with "My back hurts," "My knees hurt," and so on. The doctors would get so frustrated with her constant complaints, they'd operate on her. They wouldn't find anything physically wrong, so she'd go to another doctor and start again with different complaints. In this case, she *was* looking at herself for the cause of her misery, but she focused on her *body,* not her mind. I said to her, "From looking at your records, I realize you're doing this to get attention, to be cared for by people. I'm not going to operate on you, but if you want to come into the office, I'll help you to change and heal what is really hurting you." This shook her, woke her up to her behavior, and she admitted she needed help.

For the next six months, she came in for psychotherapy. We'd sit and talk, and slowly she got better and better. Eventually I got a letter from her insurance company saying they didn't pay surgeons for talking. I wrote back, "Look at her record this year. Look how much money you spent on her in the first six months, and then look at the last six months, how little money you had to spend. She's been doing these operations to punish herself for many crazy reasons. The talking therapy is changing how she feels about herself, and she isn't hurting anymore." I got such a kick out of the next letter they sent to me. It said, "Alright, keep talking."

Changing our lives might require making big decisions or little adjustments. Sometimes we need to change our environment, while at other times we need to change our attitudes, perspectives, or behavior. Two good questions to ask are these: Do I have a sense of fulfillment from my work and daily activities? Am I happy in my family and other relationships? If the answer to either of these is no, it may be a sign that you need to make some changes in your life. Your mental, physical, and spiritual health depends on you making the right choices.

If you don't like your life, change it. Move, quit, leave the partner, get help. Don't fear change—change fear. When you see it as a labor of love for the person your Highest Self desires you to be, change becomes less frightening. I asked some cancer patients to write a poem about rebirthing themselves. One gentleman expressed it beautifully in the last lines of his poem:

Two of me as yet, but one will fade
—that guy who thought he would live forever—
and out of him this other's being made,
not perfect either,
but worth all the endeavor.

If you are tempted to place the blame for your frustration and unhappiness upon others, look instead to Confucius and the archer. Perhaps the fault lies only in the choices you made. I encourage you to write a description of your ideal life and put it in the beginning of your journal, your life manual. Look at it often and imagine yourself in that life. You have the right to be happy. Go ahead—become your own agent of change!

Change Your Heart to Change Your Attitude

Nothing in the world is as soft and yielding as water, yet for dissolving the hard and inflexible, nothing can surpass it. The soft overcomes the hard; the gentle overcomes the rigid.

– **Lao-tzu** (601–Unknown B.C.),
Chinese philosopher and author of Tao Te Ching

When our attitudes develop from childhood, they can become as solid as rock, but that doesn't make them permanent. Have you ever observed the boulders beneath a waterfall? Over time, their hard surface yields under the constant pounding of water; sharp edges soften into curves, and the eroding force can even create grooves. Our habitual thoughts are just the same. Repeating any thought, whether it is a negative or a positive one, will make your body respond as if that thought were true. No matter what stance you adopt, all your life circumstances will mirror your thoughts and beliefs, thus creating your reality.

Forty years ago, I had trouble getting anybody to study the connection between people's lives and their health or loss of health. But today scientists are studying epigenetics: the interplay between environment and DNA or genes. They now recognize how much genes affect people's lives and how people's lives affect genes in turn. It isn't the gene making the decision; it's the person's thoughts and attitudes that act like a light switch. All genes have an on switch and an off switch, each one producing a different effect. When you constantly think, *Oh, I hate my job; my life is so difficult*, your attitude becomes that of a powerless victim. Your genes respond in a way that supports being a victim. If you don't like your life, you won't deal well with environmental toxins, stress, or disease because you've told your body that death is better than living like this. Long-term, constant stress can even change your DNA. Not only does this reduce your ability to adapt to stressors, but the genetic mutation or defect can pass on to the next generation. On the other hand, if you love your life, your genes get the opposite message, and they respond vigorously to keep you healthy and alive.

One of my medical students did a study comparing actors who were performing in a serious drama versus those in a comedy. All the actors were dealing with the same stresses: learning lines, appearing night after night, and playing to audiences and critics. Over the winter, many of the drama actors were catching colds and flu and had to drop out while they recovered. Playing unhappy characters was affecting their immune systems. At the same time, actors in the comedy weren't getting sick. They were experiencing the joys of life—the fun and the laughter. Their bodies responded to the laughter and joy by building stronger immune systems.

Your thoughts, not the circumstances you are in, are what make you happy or unhappy. Believe it or not, you can change your thoughts merely by changing how you word them. Try this experiment: Say out loud, "I *have to* pay my bills." Now, close your eyes; repeat the thought, and pay attention to your body. How did *having to* pay your bills make you feel? Maybe you started to frown, clenched your teeth, or tensed your shoulder muscles. Perhaps you felt worried and powerless.

Now say out loud, "I *get to* pay my bills." Close your eyes again. Repeat the thought and listen to your body. Did you stop frowning? Did your jaw and shoulders relax? Has your mood changed from worry to relief or gratitude? Start listening to the language you use on a daily basis, and change any words that take away your choice. You don't *have to* do anything, but you *get to* do everything, if you choose. Sometimes it only takes a change of words from "I *should* do this" to "I *could* do this." It is also okay to say, "I *won't* do this."

When something is disturbing your happiness, don't be rigid as a rock. Ask yourself what thoughts you are willing to give up happiness for. As Jesus said to Nicodemus, we are water and spirit. Be yielding, and let your thoughts reshape you like the boulder beneath the waterfall. Take back your power and adopt a grateful attitude. It works for me when I think about paying bills for our kids and tuition for our grandchildren. When I do it out of love and gratitude, the chance to help them becomes a reward for me.

Many people make themselves unhappy because they insist on winning, being successful, or being perfect. They consider themselves failures when that doesn't happen. If you change your negative attitude about achieving what you intended into a lesson that helps you do better next time, you are less likely to repeat mistakes, and you'll forge new ways of achieving your goals. You won't waste time hating yourself or hating the steps that made you wiser and more knowledgeable. Your shining example will also inspire and teach others, sharing the key to success.

A person's attitude toward life itself has a lot to do with survival because attitude creates physiological changes in the body. It is well documented that optimists live longer than pessimists, and they enjoy life much more. Optimism breeds life, while despair and hopelessness kill. Asking people the question "Do you want to live to be 100?" can reveal their attitudes toward life and their survival behavior. Are you afraid to live and grow older, or do you look forward to the opportunities life presents as you age? We all grow older, but only some of us grow old.

I love giving people a pin with the word *ATTITUDE* on it. It makes a good talking point and reminds them to be aware of how they affect themselves and everyone around them. If the person wearing it is acting out of sorts, you can point to the pin and say, "Your attitude needs straightening." They smile or laugh and get the message. It isn't rude or insulting, and it really works. Happiness is a choice.

A great teacher for me was a medical secretary who said, "When I took the job at the hospital, I hated it. I was surrounded by miserable people and all the doctors and nurses." On the same day that she took the job, she went to the office to tell them they could have their job back. They told her she couldn't just quit; she had signed a contract that required her to give two weeks' notice. She said to me, "For two weeks I got up miserable every day. On the last day, I got up happy, went to work happy, and then I noticed something. All the people around me were happy. So I didn't quit; I decided to come in happy."

When I met her, she had been working there for two years. I had given her an attitude pin for the happiness and love that she radiated around the hospital and the affect she had on everyone. It was then that she told me her story. What a great example she was of a change agent. Another time she received a pin with her name on it and a rainbow. I gave these to any employee I saw really caring for someone. I also handed out cards that said, "Laughter is contagious. Be a carrier." By focusing on the positives, we created a hospital club of special people.

Happiness isn't a gift we're born with; it's an active choice, *a participation in positivity.* The difference in happy people is that they have made a choice about how they are willing to think, to react, and to spend their time. When you show up happy, everyone feels happier.

Remember, everyone around you is living the same human life you are. We all have our troubles and difficulties. So when you feel the world is a place of unfairness and darkness, change your life, or change your attitude toward your life. Flip the switch from down to up, and brighten your outlook. Be a change agent for yourself, and you'll become a lighthouse for those around you.

Think about the miraculous properties of water: rock hard when frozen, soft and flowing in liquid form, and free as a spirit when boiled into vapor. Seventy-three percent of your brain is composed of water. If your attitude is ice-solid and you can't change it, remember Lao Tzu, the Chinese philosopher. Ponder the properties of water, and then *soften up*. You'll be surprised at how easy change is.

Try a Different Perspective

When you stand in front of me and look at me, what do you know of the griefs that are in me and what do I know of yours. And if I were to cast myself down before you and weep and tell you, what more would you know about me than you know about hell when someone tells you it is hot and dreadful. For that reason alone we human beings ought to stand before one another as reverently, as reflectively, as lovingly, as we would before the entrance to hell.

– **Franz Kafka** (1883-1924),
Jewish novelist and major figure
of 20th-century literature

Kafka's statement applies to any place or circumstance, whether we're dealing with people, animals, or the earth, because he's talking about perspective. I believe all medical students should spend a week in a hospital bed in order to experience the perspective of patients. If doctors, nurses, and administrators knew first-hand what it feels like to lose their freedom, privacy, and dignity while trying to get well in a noisy, uncomfortable place—away from home and loved ones—they'd be more compassionate. They would treat patients as human beings, not diagnoses, bed occupants, or room numbers. One of the leading causes of death in hospitals is medical error, such as people being given a treatment not intended for them by a member of staff who is treating a room number or a disease rather than a patient with a name and body.

A college assignment called the Immersion Experience was given to California counseling students. For one day, students were to put themselves in the shoes of someone with physical or social challenges. They chose a variety of challenging life circumstances to adopt for a day. Some of them wrapped weighted pads around their knees and elbows, wore thick gloves and glasses to make everything blurry, and plugged their ears, reducing their ability to hear. They were then given a shopping list and instructions to bring the items back to class. Other students were blindfolded and taken by a trusted person to an unknown place, where they had to walk in public with only their guide's elbow and voice to help them navigate. The padded, lensed, and muffled students experienced the difficulties of the elderly when trying to read small-print labels, fish change out of pockets and purses, open heavy doors, carry bags up staircases, follow verbal instructions, and so on. Blindfolded students discovered that when they asked for directions, people shouted as if they were deaf, or they pointed where to go when the student obviously couldn't see. As people walked past the blindfolded students and their sighted guides, the blind students became aware of passersby exchanging glances with their guides in a silent conversation—an exchange they were not part of. It left them feeling isolated and cut off from the enjoyment of others. Students who spent the day in wheelchairs experienced the insulting frustration of people talking over their heads to the people accompanying them.

Having gained a new perspective, the students expressed that they now had more compassion, patience, and a greater appreciation for the courage of people who live with such challenges every day. To paraphrase Kafka's beautiful sentiment, they could now "stand before one another as reverently, as reflectively, as lovingly" as they would wish others to stand before them.

A change of perspective can be used to help any situation or circumstance. Robert Schuller, the minister, was scheduled to give a lecture on success to a group of businessmen. But it had been a terrible year, and just before delivering his lecture, he was told *not* to speak on success. Schuller was taken aback, but as he went up to the lectern, a thought came to him: tough times don't last, but tough people do. By giving these businessmen a different perspective, he inspired everyone with a new mind-set for success.

Recently my co-author, Cynthia, had to face one of her greatest fears. Changing her perspective pulled her through it. She wrote:

I didn't know what we were getting into as my dogs and I climbed a steep hill through woods we hadn't visited before. About half a mile up the rocky trail, the path narrowed considerably and in some places, there was a sheer drop-off on one side. Eventually we came to a hole where recent rains had washed the path out, leaving a trail of rocks and wet soil hundreds of feet below. So the dogs and I turned around and began our return trek down the hill.

When we reached the spot where the path narrowed to less than a foot, I glanced over the steep edge. Without warning, a wave of dizziness and nausea struck me. My heart began to race, and I felt like I couldn't breathe. I froze then and could not move for fear of falling. With no other footprints on the path than ours, I knew there was little chance of anyone coming to the rescue. I had to make the descent on my own accord.

I prayed for help. Immediately a thought came to me: Be an ant. I focused on the 10-inch-wide trail and imagined myself seeing through the eyes of an ant. Seeing the world from an ant's perspective changed everything. The path suddenly widened to the equivalent of a six-lane highway! I took a step forward, followed by another and another. My body relaxed, and the nausea and dizziness went away. With new confidence I made it safely down the hill, the dogs and I in a gloriously happy state.

As Cynthia's story shows, a small adjustment in one's perspective can make a huge difference. Another example of this came from the hospital where I practiced. Four chemotherapy drugs with the first letters E, P, O, and H were given as the "EPOH Protocol" to cancer patients. One doctor turned the letters around to the "HOPE Protocol" and had more patients respond positively to the treatment. If this doctor had no reverence for his patients, he wouldn't have bothered to see things from their perspective and feed them a positive message along with the drug. This story beautifully illustrates how powerful genuine reverence is.

Whenever you face some difficulty, look at it from a different point of view. Changing your perspective on circumstances opens the door to new opportunities and greater achievements. The next time you are responsible for someone's treatment or care, remember Kafka's words: "What do you know of the griefs that are in me and what do I know of yours?" Educate yourself on how other people experience the world by being in their shoes for a day. When we do this, we are equipped to be of real help and to spread hope in a loving, respectful way.

Move from Mind to Heart

Seek goodness everywhere, and when it is found, bring it out of its hiding place and let it be free and unashamed. . . . Discover in all things that which shines and is beyond corruption. Ignore the obvious, for it is unworthy of the clear eye and the kindly heart.

– **WILLIAM SAROYAN** (1908-1981),
ARMENIAN-AMERICAN NOVELIST, PLAYWRIGHT,
AND SHORT STORY WRITER

Often when we perform a kindness for someone, we do it surreptitiously, as if it is something to be ashamed of. That's crazy! Humans and animals learn by watching the actions of others. When you see an act of kindness, you are more likely to repeat that behavior. Prime time news programs designate a disproportionately high coverage to crimes and violence compared to upbeat stories about loving, helpful kindnesses people have done for others. I wish they turned their programming around, dedicating the majority of time to good news.

At least you don't need to add to the world's misery. Give the world a boost. Let people see your acts of kindness, empathy, and generosity. When you "bring it out of its hiding place," you discover your authentic self—you feel with your heart and see through your "clear eye."

Any time you are perplexed about a situation or have a problem with somebody, set your mind aside. Listen instead to what your heart tells you, for the heart *always* seeks goodness. Once your path points in the direction of your heart's compass, you can use your mind as a beneficial tool to help you on your journey.

Often we can't feel the message of our hearts because our thinking is where we live most of the time. Thoughts can corrupt us—they shout over the heart's voice, especially when we're focusing on what is outside of us—when we're not minding our own business. What do I mean by that? A friend of mine says there are three kinds of business: God's business, other people's business, and your business. You cannot control the weather—that's God's business. You can't control the actions or thoughts of others. Even what they think about *you* is their business, not yours. Only *your* feelings, thoughts, and actions are your business, your area of control. When you stop minding your business, you step away from your heart's voice.

Agitation is a good indicator that you are in your mind, not your heart. Anytime you feel agitated or unhappy, ask yourself, "Whose business am I in?" Then step back. By removing the distraction of what we cannot control, and by listening to our hearts instead, we make the right decision, behave the right way, and our peace of mind returns.

I loved reading Saroyan's plays and stories because he understood what "the right mind" is and what living from your heart means. But what did he mean by "ignore the obvious"? Let me ask you a question. A man is sitting in a doorway, sheltered from the rain, his clothes crumpled and dirty, hands unwashed. In his pocket you can plainly see a half-consumed bottle of whiskey. As you walk past him, he asks for money to buy some food. What are you going to do? Will you focus on the bottle of whiskey, judge him, ignore him, and keep walking? Or will you ask him what kind of sandwich he'd like and then go and buy one for him? The first option is logical. But the second one shines because it comes from the heart. While you're buying that sandwich, let the cashier know you're feeding the guy in the street who has no money for food. Give others a chance to be inspired by your act of kindness.

Your next act of kindness could literally save someone's life. One example of this happened late one night when a London bus driver let a passenger on board even though he had no fare money. The driver knew the obvious—don't give free rides—but he saw with clear eyes the person's distress and listened to his heart instead. As the bus pulled away from the curb, the driver noticed a knife-wielding street gang approaching the corner, looking for trouble. If he had followed company rules and refused his penniless passenger, he realized, the gang would have had their victim. His simple action of kindness saved one person's life and inspired another passenger, who witnessed it and told me the story.

Hate is a form of corruption. It comes from fear, and fear happens when you live in your mind. I believe when you hate others, you hate yourself and your life. When you stop hating yourself, you will not hate others—you will understand them. When you love yourself, you become able to love another. And guess what? Science is now verifying the fact that it is good for you to love. You live a healthier and longer life. Imagine that.

Many years ago, I asked the anthropologist Ashley Montagu how I could become a more loving person. This was a genuine desire on my part to change. He said, very simply, "Act as if you are a loving person." I asked him what he meant on a practical level, and he said, "If you are having difficulty with someone, when that person comes into the room, think about how you would behave if you loved that person, and then act as if you do." I began to do that, and it helped enormously. Acting from my heart not only changed me, it also affected the people in my life, who were now experiencing that love.

When you run into angry people, be what I call a Love Warrior. I find that love is a potent weapon. People who grow up with criticism, complaints, shouting, and fighting become confused when you don't behave the same in return. I have been able to stop violent people from doing any harm to me and others by telling them, "I love you." Our children were afraid of what was going to happen to me when I approached a violent, cursing young man and said those words. I added, "I am sorry your parents don't." His reaction was to become silent, turn, and leave. When a psychotic man began screaming at me in the emergency room, I said to him, "I love you." He stopped screaming and quietly returned to his cubicle.

Saroyan also advised us to "seek goodness." This means to not only notice it when it happens, but also ask people to bring it about. You'll be amazed how folks respond when you ask them to reach for the goodness in their hearts. One time, Bobbie and I were having difficulty getting our carry-on luggage accepted on a plane. The attendant said it wouldn't fit, but the size was only bordering on too large. I sought the goodness in her and said, "I need your love." Immediately the attendant changed from her mind to her heart and let me carry the luggage on.

Even when somebody consciously wishes to harm you, look for the goodness in them. In Dostoevsky's story "The Grand Inquisitor," the Inquisitor orders a new stranger in the town to be jailed, for the people believe this stranger is the returned Christ. He had been performing miracles of healing in front of everyone. The old Inquisitor goes into the prisoner's cell, rants at him, taunts him, and threatens to have him burned at the stake. Rather than fight or argue with the old man, the prisoner listens quietly and looks gently into his eyes. The Inquisitor longs for the stranger to put up some defense or prove him wrong. But the prisoner is not defensive. Instead, he approaches the old man and softly kisses him on his "bloodless aged lips." This simple, loving act woke the Inquisitor's sleeping heart, for he opened the cell door and told the prisoner to never come back.

When Norman Vincent Peale died in his 90s, one of his mourners said that he outlived his critics. Another person responded, "No, he out-loved them." If you want to upset your critics, don't *think* about them; *love* them. Remember, when you live in your mind, you are constantly arguing, weighing, and comparing. The next time you are faced with a troubled person or threatening situation, do as Saroyan says—be unashamed to let your heart out of hiding. When you live in your heart, seeking only that which shines, magic happens.

OUT OF MY MIND

I am usually out of my mind
There is nowhere else
I'd rather come from
Or go to
Or be
Sometimes I get iost in my thoughts
I struggle to find my way out
Out of my mind
And into my body
So I can feel
And find my way into my heart
And my right mind

SEEK THE CREATOR EVERYWHERE

Apprehend God in all things,
For God is in all things.
Every single creature is full of God
And is a book about God.
Every creature is a word of God.

– **Meister Eckhart** (1260–1328),
German philosopher, theologian, and mystic

What Eckhart is saying is that we are, in a real sense, God learning about God. We are students from the day we're born until the day we die, and the *only subject* is God. Our life is about learning to understand creation and the Creator, for we are co-creating the universe every moment we're alive.

When we graduate from high school, college, or university, we don't know that *life* is the *real* classroom. You've studied all the textbooks, passed the exams, and received your degree, and you think things will be smooth sailing from now on. But life isn't like that. Life throws things at you—and not just one at a time. A sentence in one of my old journals makes me laugh. It says, "And then your cat goes into heat." Just when it seems everything is in turmoil—that it can't get any worse—your cat goes into heat, rolling around the house, making all that racket, and driving everybody crazy. So take it from me: even if you think you've learned your lessons and got all your problems solved, there is always something else to learn, something waiting to happen.

As Meister Eckhart suggested, *apprehend the lesson*, for God is in all things, including the lessons! There is a saying that when the student is ready, the teacher appears. I would add to that: and the teacher appears in unexpected, but appropriate, guises. Sometimes the teacher is a stranger you meet on the street. Years ago, Bobbie and I were hoofing it through a street in San Francisco, a little late for a meeting. A homeless lady stood on the steps of a building asking passersby for change. Because of the hurry we were in, we walked by without stopping. I felt guilty about not fishing out my wallet, and as we passed her, I said, "I'm sorry; we are a little late, and don't have time to stop." She mumbled something, and my sense was that she was criticizing me for not giving her any money. I went over to her, ready for an argument, and asked, "What did you say?" She replied, very simply, "You don't have to be sorry." I felt the burden of guilt lifted from me, just as if she were God and had said, "Your sins are forgiven." What kindness and humility she displayed. I learned the lesson, and now I always make time to give the gift.

Teachers and prophets exist everywhere and in every experience. They come from different cultures and countries, in various sizes and species, and each one is truly a mirror of God, or, as Eckhart puts it, "a book about God." When we listen to them, we are studying God, and they speak to us only when God knows we're ready. So take time as you go through your day to observe and listen. When you learn something important—some truth or wisdom that helps you to grow—write it down in your Bible II. Life contains many precious opportunities for you to study, experiment, engage, and grow. Be conscious that you are a student of life, a creature of God, a word of God. All that exists around you—and in you—is your classroom, the classroom of your soul.

Turn to Nature

Just ask the animals, and they will teach you.
Ask the birds of the sky, and they will tell you.
Speak to the earth, and it will instruct you.
Let the fish in the sea speak to you.

– **Job 12:7-8**,
New Living Translation

If Jesus doesn't fit for you, let the great outdoors be your teacher. I realized long ago how much I could learn by observing nature and how she deals with adversity. Nature doesn't charge for therapy, either. She sustains us and speaks to us. Her cycles and rhythms appear through light, movement, and sounds: lapping waves, tumbling stones, pulsing sap of plants and trees—all mimicking the rhythms inside our bodies. Even the quaking earth, in periodic thrusts of volcanic labor, speaks to the heart of us and our nature.

I love to go walking or jogging in the morning. The exercise does a lot for me physically and psychologically. It establishes the rhythm of my day while I experience nature and gather my thoughts in quiet solitude. I began this practice many years ago, and I found that voices would speak to me while I ran. Many times I "felt" the voices of animals, trees, rocks, or weather. Just as the rain falls on the earth and becomes a flower, the voice can enter you and become conscious. In nature there is a continuity of consciousness.

Sometimes I heard the voices of my patients or members of my cancer support group who were dying and saying good-bye. I didn't always know the name of the person; at times it was just a sense of something being communicated to me, saying, "I'm leaving, good-bye." When I got home, a phone call would confirm what I had heard or felt as I ran. I would share these messages with Bobbie because she knew many of the people I worked with.

One day on my run, the spirit of Bobbie's mother appeared to me and said good-bye. I went straight to her nursing home, knowing she had died. When I walked in, the nurse said, "Oh, you heard."

"No, I didn't hear, but I know," I replied. My experiences in nature and the voices I heard reinforced the lesson that life never ends, and that love and consciousness are the only reality.

Order in nature does not mean perfection—it means balance and harmony, which include storms and darkness as well as sunshine and warm breezes. I have seen a tree grow around a barbed wire fence, teaching me to embrace the irritations and difficulties in my life. I see the dead becoming part of the earth again, feeding and supporting the living in a constant cycle of beginnings and no endings. I have learned a lot by just walking through the snow: how previous footprints can help at times so we don't have to struggle. We can follow in another's footprints, and yet those same footprints may be frozen, unyielding, and troublesome. This is when one needs to make his own way, create a new path and set of footprints.

We can learn from nature's metaphors. When we start something new and add to it—what may seem insignificant, such as one's belief or one's faith—persistent growth and beautiful things will happen. Just as the seed grows, so do you.

My work with cancer patients is a good example. Years ago, I started a support group for people with cancer called Exceptional Cancer Patients, or ECaP. The seed of my idea was a specific form of individual and group therapy that utilized patients' drawings, dreams, images, and feelings. It is based on "carefrontation," a safe, loving, therapeutic confrontation that facilitates personal lifestyle changes, personal empowerment, and healing of the individual's life. From that small seed of a beginning have come many books, videos, and podcasts. These acted like ripples on water—spreading seeds of hope around the world, helping millions of people to heal their lives and recover their health.

In his book *The Power of One,* Bryce Courtenay talks about a troubled young boy who is told to go to nature for the answers to his problems. The boy comes upon a waterfall, stops to observe, and notices that the waterfall starts with one drop at a time. If he wants to change, he only needs to make one positive move to begin the process. The boy also realizes the power contained in many drops of water, the same as we have when we all come together—the power of one. Nature inspired the boy to go forward in the face of adversity.

Another one of nature's lessons came from a native plant in our area. A few years ago, the road where I jog was repaved. Over the next days, I noticed a crack forming in the pavement, and soon a skunk cabbage emerged. It was incredible to me that a tender shoot could overcome such a heavy, hard surface to reach daylight. Its persistence became for me a metaphor for faith. This plant didn't look at the statistics and question what its chances were. It just kept pushing upward, using its sense of gravity with no warmth or sunlight to guide it. After photographing the shoot, I brought Bobbie down to see it. She said, "Honey, it is just a skunk cabbage."

"Yes, it is just an ordinary skunk cabbage," I said, "and a miracle too."

I used to show a slide of that skunk cabbage at my talks. One night someone handed me a poem. No author was noted. The poem finished with the following lines:

The happy skunk cabbage is vivid with earth;
malodorous, vulgar, impenitent, broad;
most tanged of the chlorophyll children of God.
Green hands in green pockets,
he loafs in the sun and contemplates earth
while the good hours run, saying:
Take me or leave me, and bless me or damn,
I am equal to God—for I am what I am!

I recall a school teacher in Oregon who was so busy she didn't take care of her garden or her life. One day she saw with dismay that her artichoke had wilted, so she discarded it in the garbage can. But the next time she lifted the lid she discovered that, instead of dying, the plant was growing there in the can. Feeling guilty, she rescued it and took it to the art teacher who had a green thumb. Shortly thereafter, she learned she had cancer. The woman began to confront her life, her mortality, and her ability to survive.

While she was in the hospital, her husband brought her the artichoke. It was in full blossom and planted in a pot that the art teacher had painted. Her class had been using the plant as a still-life model when its beautiful purple blossoms burst forth. During its time under the garbage can lid, the discarded artichoke had never asked if there was any point in blossoming or if anybody was going to see it. It just went on being what it was meant to be—*I am what I am*. The artichoke helped that school teacher to go on being what she was meant to be, and its valuable lesson prolonged her life.

I would advise you to present your problems and questions to nature and observe what's in front of you. Let the ordinary skunk cabbages and artichokes be your miracles, your teachers. Visit the woods. Walk along the riverbank, or trek through the desert. Do as it says in the Book of Job: listen to the ocean and let her creatures inform you. Let the birds be your messengers and inspiration. Turn to nature and be comforted, for God's presence is right there beside you.

Learn from the Animals

[The eyes of the animal] contain the truth of life, an equal sum of pain and pleasure, the capacity for joy and the capacity for suffering. . . . When God made animals, He equipped them with just those needs and impulses that enable them to live according to their laws. We assume that He has done the same with man. In a way the animal is more pious than man, because it fulfills a divine will more completely than man ever can dream of.

– **Carl Gustav Jung**

I agree with Jung, for the animal knows its soul, I think, better than man. Think about that. As the Bible tells us, God didn't give directions to the animals but did to Adam. And the Bible says that after God put animals on the earth, he saw that *they* were good, but it doesn't say that about man. Animals don't get into the intellectual difficulties we do; they don't filter their feelings or mask the truth of who they are. Neither do they have the freedom of choice we enjoy, so they live according to their laws of nature. Man does not live according to the laws of nature and God. Our freedom challenges us with the potential to be godlike and make our lives meaningful, but animals are already living this quality and giving their love without judgment.

I came across an article in a medical journal written 100 years ago. It was questioning who is wiser, man or brute. The physician listed the choices we make with our diets, drinking, smoking, and other habits, and he compared them to animal behavior. The obvious conclusion was that the brute is wiser. We call it horse sense.

One day, as I was jogging, I saw ahead of me what looked like two big dogs. As I ran closer, I realized it was two deer: a doe and her fawn. Upon seeing me, the doe leaped into the woods, but the fawn seemed thoroughly intrigued by me. I saw all of creation in her eyes as she stood there, a beautiful creature with no fear. She looked at me with as much curiosity and interest as I did her. I went home and told everybody about this incredible moment when a fawn and I stood a few feet apart, looking into each other's eyes. I imagined the fawn going back to her family, just like I had, reporting, "Hey, I saw this bizarre creature running on two legs." She became a symbol for me of the connections between us all, and how *just being ourselves* makes us a gift to all others.

My co-author Cynthia used to volunteer every Saturday at a wild bird sanctuary, feeding rescued baby birds on the dawn shift. She writes:

On my first day I was shown the room where rescued birds, from hours-old chicks to fledglings, were kept in incubators or laundry baskets with netting over the top. Someone had left the net unsecured on one of the baskets, and while we did the rounds, a young thrush got out. It began a clumsy flight around the room and was in danger of hurting itself or escaping if someone opened the door. As it flew over my head, I reached up and caught it! What an amazing feeling—wild bird in my hand, its heart beating against my palm and warm claws clasping my ring finger for support. I was hooked from that moment. For the next two years my Saturdays belonged to the birds.

One morning at the height of nesting season, I arrived to the cacophony of 80 hungry birds, all of them desperate for their first meal of the day. I did the rounds as fast as I could, starting with the incubator chicks who needed feeding every 20 minutes or they could die. When finished with them, I moved to the older chicks and read the card pinned to the first basket. It registered two towhees inside, but I only saw one, so I guessed someone had made a mistake.

I syringed some water into the towhee's throat before feeding it some protein mash, followed by three lively mealy worms. When he took the fourth worm, he didn't swallow it, but held on. He tilted his head and kept staring into my eyes; I

> felt certain he was trying to communicate something. But I needed to move on to the next bird, so I put the towhee back in the basket. At this point, he dropped the mealy worm. I retrieved the worm and offered it to him. Once again, he held the squiggly thing in his beak without eating it, tilted his head, and stared at me as if trying to tell me something. The towhee then hopped to the far corner of the basket, where the netting had bunched into folds. Suddenly another baby bird's head popped out from the folds, and my little towhee began feeding him the worm! The smaller chick's foot had become caught in the material, completely hiding him. With so many birds to feed, I would not have made it round to this basket again for an hour or more.
>
> I was overcome with awe at this vulnerable little creature that had trusted me to do my job, and when I didn't, took the responsibility upon himself. His demanding eyes, which had kept me there, literally contained the gift of life for another bird. If one wild orphan can show such care for his little brother, how can we see others in need and turn our heads away?

Cynthia's lesson on God's nature, expressed and taught by an innocent wild bird, is only one of many examples where animals show love to their fellow creatures, even to species not of their own. I have often told of the butterfly that Bobbie rescued when we were in Hawaii, how it refused to leave her, staying on her shoulder no matter what we did. I realized the spirit of a dear friend who had gone back to Hawaii to die had entered the butterfly's body, because it stayed with us all night. In the morning it allowed me to put it in a paper bag, bring it to the outdoor workshop I was giving, and release it as a symbol of rebirth. The butterfly fluttered and circled around us for the rest of the day and did not fly away until the workshop was over. As if acting upon the truth of Jung's words, this pious little creature fulfilled a divine will—illustrating God's lesson. The caterpillar bursts from its spent cocoon to become a beautiful winged creature, and we too become free, transformed, and perfect in death, when our consciousness leaves the body behind.

Many people are more in love with their animals than with themselves. I would like you to do something very simple: treat yourselves as well as you treat your beloved animals. Pets have often been raised with loving parenting, little criticism, and few rules. They have no school grades or religions to make them feel judged. If we did the same, it would solve many of the world's problems. Studies show that if you have a pet, your survival rate is significantly higher than that of people with the same disease and no pet in the house. I have stopped family members of patients from getting rid of the patients' pets when the patients are too sick to care for them. Taking the pets away removes the patient's motivation to get better and live. If you really want to help your loved ones recover, clean their house and feed their pets.

What have you learned from the animals in your life? If you don't have a pet, get one. Whenever you have doubts about how to behave, look to your pets and see what they do, for as Jung says, they are more complete in God's eyes, fulfilling divine will in a way we can only dream of. Let the pious professors in their coats of feather, fur, and scales be your teachers. Allow them to enrich your soul with wisdom, love, laughter, and joy.

Listen to the Voice

*Your ears will hear a voice behind you, saying,
"This is the way; walk in it."*

– **Isaiah 30:21**,
New International Version

I began hearing voices early in my life, and what they have communicated to me has been an incredible gift. There is a voice that speaks to me continuously and directs me to deeply meaningful places and experiences. It also tells me what to say in lectures and more. Bobbie always said, "It comes from God-knows-where."

Where does this voice come from? It comes from the nothingness, the indescribable, undifferentiated, abstract potential from which all creation occurs. When our universe was formed, we had energy and matter. Then intelligence came, along with information and the ability to transmit it by messenger molecules. Nerves came later as bodies were created. We all, whether animate, mineral, or gas, share the ability to respond to these messenger molecules. Energy, matter, thoughts, and information are all part of one system, one consciousness, one universe.

When people hear God's voice, the first thought they have is that they have gone crazy or that somebody is tricking them. But the voice is real. Isaiah recognized that, just as prophets and psychics have realized for centuries. Whether you believe it is the voice of your Creator, your intuition, an angel, or some kindly spirit doesn't matter. I encourage you to listen *for* it and *to* it. Don't be afraid. As long as its message is a loving one, you can trust it. If the message doesn't feel truthful or loving, be careful. If it is hateful toward you or others—or directs you to do harm to yourself or anyone else—it is a sign of a mental disorder. If that happens, you should speak to your doctor and get help as soon as you can.

There are many who talk to, shout at, or pray to God, but when He responds, they don't accept it as real—they shun the very answer they were seeking. Others are so skeptical they can't hear the voice, which only acts to prove that their skepticism was well founded. Recently I read about a man who got lost in the Arctic. He was telling his friends that he prayed for help, "but God didn't do anything. God didn't save me." One of the friends said, "But here you are—you were saved!" The skeptic replied, "No, an Inuit came along; *he* showed me the way." The Inuit's appearance was no coincidence. Knowing the skeptic would neither listen to nor believe His voice,

God communicated instead with someone accustomed to trusting what he heard and felt. The Inuit let the voice guide him until he found the lost man. Many of the world's native peoples understand that the great consciousness is always working for us.

God often uses people as his instrument. A dying child once asked me, "Why am I different?" Before I even had a chance to take that in, I heard my voice respond, "Because it makes you beautiful." I knew it wasn't me who spoke. That answer wasn't one I would even think of. I recognized it as the voice of my angel using me and my body to speak for him. At first I was concerned the boy would be upset with me for saying it. Instead, a beautiful smile appeared on his face. He knew his differences did make him very special and unique. He created a lot of beauty in the world and helped many people with his disease, before and after he died. As a matter of fact, that boy, Tony Fenton, is still honored and remembered by various fundraising efforts for cystic fibrosis.

Not hearing the voice does not mean there is something wrong with you or that you are not capable. Celestial silence is not punishment; it is simply that you are unable to hear above the roar of your internal noise. You need to be still and quiet to hear. But also try listening to the voice when the five children around you are creating a commotion or people are making demands on you where you work. It *is* possible they are speaking for God at times, trying to keep you focused on your heart, when you are thinking and not feeling. Be open to listening to the voice *and* its spokespersons. Always thank them for helping you.

Sometimes I resented all the noise and chaos around me in the hospital, in the house, on the road—everywhere I went. One day, wishing I could escape and just walk on the beach, I sat down and began to write the following poem. By the time I had finished, I realized God was talking to me just through the act of writing.

SILENCE

Fax, phone, mail, life
Whose home is this?
What do they all want?
Where is the silence?
I remember hearing nothing
Surrounded by sand dunes and nature
God, how beautiful and deafening is silence
It drowns out the fax, phones, and mail
Silence is so loud

Nothing can or need be heard

I need to be silent *inside*

Until I can return

To the silence outside

To hear it all

God talks to everyone. You don't have to belong to a specific religion, have special gifts, or possess psychic ability. Express your thoughts and feelings, and hand your needs over to God. He is there for you when you knock on His door. Often He will provide a sign confirming you've been heard. Remember, there is nothing wrong with dialogue—maybe the next voice God needs to hear is yours. Don't be afraid to get your Lord's attention with talk, humor, song, creative expression, or prayer. God needs us in order to complete creation.

I met a gentleman who told me that once he was flying a small private plane when something happened to the engine. He knew he was going to crash. He didn't expect to survive this, and as the plane descended, his whole life passed before him. But a voice said to him, "You will be alright." And that voice stayed with him and comforted him. The man did crash and survived with facial injuries and the loss of an eye. The rest of his body was not injured at all.

I have heard and read about many similar stories. One that I came across in *Guideposts* magazine related the experience of a man and his friend, who were flying. It was pitch dark, the engine was failing, and they couldn't get back to the airport they had just left. A voice told the man to go straight ahead and land. He followed the instruction and landed safely in an open field, missing wires and other dangers.

Another time a man at the post office told me he had just been sitting in his car, screaming at God for all the difficulties he was going through in his life. When he finished his outburst and all his pain and despair were spent, a card fell off the visor onto the front seat beside him. He had no idea where the card came from or how long it had been there. He then handed it to me. On one side was a spiritual symbol which he said brought him a feeling of peace and healing. On the reverse were printed the words "Fear not, for I am with you. Do *not* be dismayed, for I *am* your God. I will strengthen you and help you. —Isaiah 41:10."

When we are in the rhythm of life, we create a state of openness, our antenna is up, and we can hear in a way that we've never heard before. In order to fulfill our unique destinities, we all need to take time on a regular basis to quiet our minds so we can become aware of the voice and the direction we are receiving. But the voice seldom comes at joyful moments. It usually comes when difficulties arise and you go beyond your own resources. It is when you have nothing left—when you turn inside yourself to look for help—that the voice that gives you strength is heard. Think of a large pond as a gusty squall whips up waves and turbulence, and as you sit there quietly, the storm passes. When the wind stops, the turbulence settles, and the water's surface becomes still. It is only in that stillness that you can see your reflection clearly. In the same way, we need a quiet mind to hear and understand God's message.

Whether you call the voice God, intuition, or God-only-knows, it is there for all of us. When I hear it or sense it and follow its instructions—even those seemingly mundane ones, such as where to park my car or when to walk the dog—amazing things happen, from the things I find to the people or animals I meet, and they aren't coincidences. As the Bible says, I just walk on the path of my life, and a voice from behind speaks. It goes straight to my heart, as if saying, "This is the way; walk in it."

5

JUST LOVE

In the time of your life, live—so that in the wondrous time you shall not add to the misery and sorrow of the world, but shall smile to the infinite delight and mystery of it.

–William Saroyan

Years ago, Bobbie and I chose a headstone for where we would one day be buried. We had Saroyan's quote carved on the stone, for it is a motto we always tried to live by. Now it stands in a beautiful cemetery near our house as a memorial to Bobbie and her life. Its message always fills me with comfort and peace, and I hope it inspires others.

When you find yourself smiling to the infinite delight and mystery of life, I can guarantee you are living from your heart, living an expression of love. You are then in balance with God's nature. We now know that when you give love—when you act with compassion—you are physiologically changed. Interview people who act out of love, whether they do so individually or as volunteers in an organization, and you will hear them describe their feelings in words that can also be used to describe the high that a euphoric drug produces. A loving act causes the release of endorphins—neurochemicals and hormones that reduce blood pressure, increase energy, make you feel connected to others, and provide a natural high. This physiological reaction happens not only to your body and to the recipient's body but also *to the bodies of those who witness the loving act.*

Relationships with other living beings are a key factor in our health and survival. Addictive euphoric drugs cannot match the power of love, no matter how closely they mimic the feeling. They create artificial highs and destroy structures in the brain that control our ability to feel happy without drugs. True spiritual love, on the other hand, gives you a wondrous near-life experience. No drug can equal it, and the side effects are all positive ones. Make a conscious effort every day to do something kind for someone—not for praise but just for the love of it. Turn small daily efforts into a habit and become a living expression of love. Pick up litter when you're walking your dog. Respectfully approach a homeless person and start a conversation. Flash a warm smile at people when you pass them on the street and forgive the driver who cuts in front of you. Rescue the worm from the pavement and return it to a safe patch of earth. Collect stories of loving acts and include them in your Bible II. Let them be your inspiration and rejuvenation during times when you need a boost. You will soon find yourself smiling to the "infinite delight and mystery" of your life.

Love the Troubled Ones

Love is the medicine for our sick old world.
If people can learn to give and receive love,
they will usually recover from their physical
or mental illness.

– **DR. KARL MENNINGER** (1893–1990),
AMERICAN PSYCHIATRIST AND CO-FOUNDER
OF THE MENNINGER CLINIC

I agree with this statement and would add that not feeling accepted or loved during childhood causes much of the illness in "our sick old world." Just as we lose our physical health when our bodies get the wrong message, so can we lose our mental health for the same reason. The cure in both instances has a lot to do with loving our lives and feeling loved. Learning to give love to others makes our lives more meaningful, which—in turn—nurtures our self-love.

Dr. Menninger was well qualified to speak of the need for love. He came from a family of psychiatrists who advocated a new way of approaching mental health treatment for both adults and children and changed how people view the mentally ill. Partly due to his work, we now know that mental illness is a symptom—not a curse, punishment, or demonic possession. Mental and physical diseases usually have roots in childhood. Children whose parents or main caregivers are not there for them—whether the absence is emotional or physical—experience a higher rate of mental and physical illness in their adult years, and they tend to have shorter lifespans.

In today's world, difficult or troubled children and teens are treated all too quickly with antidepressants and other behavior-controlling drugs. Instead of putting them in institutions for the insane, as they did in Menninger's time, we label them with mental-behavioral disorders and place them on drugs that won't change the source of their problems and often bring on more problems.

In my pediatric and general surgery practice—and as a parent of five children—I learned a lot about loving and living from my young coaches, especially those with emotional and mental difficulties. Before children start school and become ingrained with adults' expectations—how to dress, what to say, what to do—they do what comes naturally; they do what makes them happy. If we followed this simple pattern of doing what makes us happy, our physical, mental, and emotional health would benefit. But life is complex, and it's easy to get knocked off track.

When children feel loved and safe, their first years are a wondrous time of curiosity, mystery, and delight. And when they get sad, worried, or frightened, they don't hide their feelings behind a mask. They cry or choose disruptive behaviors to exhibit what's really going on for them, trying to get the attention of adults. Even when parents do their best to love and care for their children, there are times when youngsters get lost in the difficulties of being a kid. Also, some kids are just harder to reach than others, and their parents can get lost in the frustration of not knowing what to do.

One Thanksgiving a teenage boy who was our guest took off all his clothing, sat under the table, and declared that he was a turkey. No one knew how to help this troubled kid. Many therapists had talked to him, but it had done no good. His father saw me standing in the corner smiling. After all, with five children of my own, this wasn't new to me. The father asked, "Can you help my son?"

"Yes," I replied. Now stop here, and before you read on, ask yourself what *you* would do.

First, what I did *not* do was tell the kid to get out from under the table and make himself decent. I didn't shame him, and I didn't ignore him as if he didn't matter. Instead, I took off my clothes, sat down next to the boy, and declared that I was a turkey too. I took plenty of time with him and explained that turkeys can wear underwear, socks, pants, shirts, and jackets. Slowly, I dressed him and myself, all the while being turkeys, and ultimately, showed him that turkeys can eat at the table too. It is not easy to stop being a turkey and to find who we truly are. It takes steps, changes, and someone to walk us through the process.

Sometimes we need to enter into the experience of the suffering person so they are able to feel our compassion. We can take our clothes off and be turkeys too. It's no big deal. By sharing their experience, we become natives in their territory, not tourists. You can help the wounded natives when they know you understand. After going through the process *with* this boy, not *at* him or *against* him, we cured him of his need to be a turkey. He and I continued to meet, and over time, I set him on a solid path to healing and recovery.

One of our children had a lot of trouble dealing with family life and school. He used to tell me, "Grandma called—she wants me to visit her," so I'd send him off to her house. Years later I learned Grandma never called. But his behavior was good, for he was taking care of himself. He just needed a break from all the commotion in our house and took it. He also used to hide in the closet and read books when Bobbie and I were away on vacation. His sister and brothers would cover for him, telling the adult sitters he'd gone early to school.

Our family often used humor as a way of dealing with problems. Shared laughter that is not demeaning can get the point across better than scolding or serious discussions, and when you laugh together, everyone feels they belong. Bringing our kids up this way helped them to develop a healthy sense of humor and lightened the burdens of growing up. The son who had trouble dealing with family and school responded particularly well to hilarity and developed a great sense of humor himself. Because he was the "troublemaker," we put him in the bedroom just off the kitchen, where we could keep track of him, and he kept that room right up until he left home. When he finished high school, we tried everything to encourage him to go to college, but he wouldn't go. We told him to at least get out and see the world, but he wouldn't leave home. So one day, when he was out of the house, we dismantled his bed and hid it. After dinner, he went into his bedroom, and we were all waiting for a reaction. Not a sound came out of his room. The next morning he came out, sat at the breakfast table, and said, "Thanks, my back feels much better now." We all had a good laugh. The important message got through to all of us—for him, that we loved him and felt it was time for him to leave the nest, and for us, that he just wasn't ready yet. Later, when he finally felt secure in himself, he went.

I have to share that this same son, the most difficult one to bring up, sent us an e-mail thanking us for all we did for him and the love we gave him his entire life. When I read it, I felt that Bobbie and I had won the lottery of love and life. Since I've been on my own, he calls me every night to be sure I am okay. Like all of our kids, he learned not only to receive love but also to give it. This is the greatest lesson of all.

So love the troubled and difficult kids; experience life from their point of view for a while, and show them they're not alone. Do you know anyone who feels like they don't fit into society because of a physical or mental difference? Go and sit with them for a while. Listen to them in a way that lets them know they are valued. Remember Menninger's advice—that love is the best medicine for all the world's ills. Act now to make tomorrow's world a more accepting and loving place. No matter what the problem is, love is always the best answer.

Show That You Care

If I can stop one heart from breaking,
I shall not live in vain;
If I can ease one life the aching,
Or cool one pain,
Or help one fainting robin
Unto his nest again,
I shall not live in vain.

– **EMILY DICKINSON** (1830–1886),
AMERICAN POET

Dickinson's compassion for all God's creatures and her ability to show them they matter is what gave her life meaning. We all need to give and receive compassion. Especially in the world of medicine—where people are at their most vulnerable—compassion is a beautiful gift.

A nurse with a similar heart to Dickinson's shared with me a story of his nursing home experience with an elderly disabled resident. For six years she had been confined to a wheelchair, unable to walk. Every night he put her to bed, and because of his own near-death experience, he often discussed love and forgiveness with her. One night he forgot to put her to bed and soon heard her voice bellowing down the hall: "Edward!" He went to her room and began to help her prepare for the night.

"Do you really think God forgives you for everything?"

"Yes, I do," he replied to her question.

"When I was a young woman, I stole my parents' silver and sold it so I could afford to get married. Do you think God would forgive me for that?"

"Yes, God will forgive you for that, Mrs. D."

"Then give me a kiss goodnight and go."

The next morning when he arrived at work, there was a note from the administrator, who wanted to see him in his office. "What did you tell Mrs. D. last night?"

"Why do you ask?"

"At 2 a.m. she came out of her room and, with no assistance, walked the length of the hall, put her teeth and Bible on the nurse's desk, and said, 'I don't need these anymore.' Then she went back to her room, lay down, and died."

Caring is infectious. A doctor I knew once received a letter from a young woman that made that fact abundantly clear to me. He showed me what she wrote:

> You probably won't remember me. Two years ago I was in your hospital under the care of another doctor. I lost my baby the day it was born.

That same day my doctor came in to see me, and as he left, he said, "There is a doctor here with the same surname as yours. He asked me about you after he saw your name on the board and said he would like to come in to see you, because you might be a relative. I told him you had lost your baby, and I didn't think you would want a visitor, but it was all right with me."

In a little while you came in, put your hand on my arm, and sat down for a moment beside my bed. You didn't say much of anything, but your eyes and your voice were kind, and I felt some comfort. As you sat there, I noticed that you looked tired and that the lines in your face were very deep. I never saw you again, but the nurses told me you were in the hospital practically night and day.

This afternoon I was a guest in a beautiful Chinese home here in Peking. The garden was enclosed by a high wall. On one side, surrounded by twining red and white flowers, was a brass plate. I asked someone to translate the Chinese characters engraved on its surface. They said: ENJOY YOURSELF. IT IS LATER THAN YOU THINK. I have not wanted another baby because I was still grieving for the one I lost. But on hearing those words, I decided not to wait any longer. Then, because I was thinking of my baby, I thought of you, the tired lines in your face, and

> the moment of sympathy you gave me when I so needed it. I don't know your age, but I'm sure you are old enough to be my father. Those few minutes you spent with me probably meant little or nothing to you, but they meant a great deal to a woman who was desperately unhappy and alone. So I am now presumptuous to think that I, in turn, can do something for you. Perhaps for you it is later than you think. Please forgive me, but when your work is over, on the day you get my letter, please sit down very quietly, all by yourself, and think about it.

The physician then told me the rest of his story. "Usually I sleep very well, but that night I woke a dozen times, seeing the brass plate on the Chinese wall. I called myself a silly old fool for being disturbed by a letter from a woman I could hardly remember. A voice inside me said, 'Maybe it *is* later than you think. Why don't you do something about it?'"

I went to my office next morning and told my colleagues I was going away for three months. I felt sure that everything would go to pieces, even though I had an entirely competent associate. But when I returned, I found there were just as many patients as when I left, everyone had recovered just as fast, and most of my patients didn't even know I had been away. It is humiliating to find how quickly and completely one's place is filled, but it is a healthy lesson. It was the first time I let go of work just to care for myself and my family for a while. I have continued to do that ever since."

One doctor's caring act soothed one woman's aching heart, helping her "unto [her] nest again." She, after a time, unknowingly did the same for him through her letter. As so often happens, the physician helped to heal the patient, and the patient helped to heal the physician.

Another gentleman wrote to me about his father, who had been a physician in Utah. Many times he would have to travel on horseback through the snow, risking his own life to help people. As part of his research into his father's life and work, the son talked to a guide who had accompanied the doctor when he visited people in remote areas. The guide told him of a time during a dangerous blizzard when his father went to see a woman dying of tuberculosis. The son said, "If he knew she was dying, he'd also know he couldn't do anything for her. I know he received no money for the visit." The guide revealed that his father had indeed received $1 and had given it to the guide.

"Why would my father do such a crazy act as that, risking his life in a blizzard?"

The guide answered, "I think he just wanted to let her know that somebody cared."

In my work as a camp counselor, we had a young man named Stuart who was overweight and not the best athlete. He reminded me of myself—raised in the city, short and chubby, and not very athletic. I knew how it felt to be the last kid standing when they pick teams and choose sides, so I always picked Stuart and the other troubled kids first when choosing my team. I wasn't interested in whether we won or lost, only in making these kids feel good. His parents remarked when they visited, "He never liked camp until this year." I didn't tell them what I had done—I just kept doing it. Stuart and the other young "Bernies" stayed on my team. We didn't win a baseball game all summer, but we had fun and appreciated each other.

That, I believe, is what we are all here for: the differences we can make and the care that we show. Caring is an act of love when freely and gladly given. So think of Emily Dickinson; emulate her, and do not live in vain. Feel the compassion in your heart, perform kind acts whenever you can, and let someone know you care. If one generation grew up feeling cared for, we'd all have our Garden of Eden.

Learn to Love Yourself

A friend of mine, an industrialist in a large plant in Ohio, told me that the best workmen in his plant are those who get into harmony with the rhythm of the machine on which they are working. He declares that if a worker will work in harmony with the rhythm of his machine, he will not be tired at the end of the day. He points out that the machine is an assembling of parts according to the law of God.

– **NORMAN VINCENT PEALE** (1898-1993),
AMERICAN MINISTER AND AUTHOR OF
THE POWER OF POSITIVE THINKING

Dr. Peale's quote impacted me with its simple wisdom, for it is another great example of seeing God in everything. There is a divine order in creation and in all life. When we recognize this order, we are seeing the laws of nature, the laws of God, made manifest. Just as the mechanic works in harmony with his machine by learning and accepting what it can and cannot do, and maintaining it to keep it in optimum condition, so can we apply the same principle to our lives. When we live in harmony with our bodies, our unique personalities, and our God-given nature, we tire less, suffer less, feel happier, and stay healthier. This is what self-love is—not trying to be what we aren't but learning what we are, appreciating and respecting our qualities and limitations, and taking care of ourselves as best we can.

One measure of self-love is in the choices we make for ourselves and whether those choices resonate or clash with our natures. Making choices isn't always easy, especially if we haven't had good models to learn from. In that case, we need to re-parent ourselves, seek better role models and coaches, and make new mottoes to live by. It takes time—sometimes several years—but we can do it.

I once knew a woman I will call "Rhonda" who had grown up in an abusive, alcoholic family. Not only that, but her parents and siblings had all committed suicide. Rhonda came to me suffering from scleroderma, a painful and disfiguring autoimmune disease that is treatable but not curable. Its impact on her was visible, and I could feel her disappointment in herself. Her parents' suicide had left her child's mind believing that she had failed as a child. I encouraged her to talk about her life while I just sat and listened. As she purged the painful memories, I could see the rage toward her parents and anger about her condition begin to *leave her body*. Rhonda came to realize that she couldn't hang on to the past, keep blaming what she could not change, and then expect her body to react in a positive way. She agreed to start talking therapy, which opened a new path for her. She learned how to reassemble her feelings about her life so that the pieces she was given began working for—not against—her.

Later she wrote to me: "I had no control over the parents who raised me or the experiences I was exposed to, but when I let love into my prison, it changed every negative item in it—meaning all those loveless experiences—and turned them into something meaningful." Rhonda found her true rhythm and balance and created God's harmony in her life. No longer at war with her past or her present, she accepted her life as the gift it was. Rhonda lived many decades beyond what her doctors predicted, confusing them in a wonderful way.

Do not let the destructive messages from those in your past continue to control your thoughts. Their messages act as poison and create negative emotions that we project onto others. It is easier to blame others for our emotional wounds. Until we transform our negative thoughts and beliefs, we will repel positive emotions, relationships, and opportunities.

One of my patients, a teenager who had suffered severe burns, used to come to her follow-up visits with me wearing turtlenecked, long-sleeved garments in 90-degree weather. When I asked her why, she answered, "Because I am ugly." This girl had come to hate herself. Self-hate removes all possibility of experiencing harmony and balance in your life, for it makes you work against the "rhythm of [your] machine" and the fine instruments that God gave you—your body and your life. One summer I helped her to get a job at a nursing home working as a nurse's aide. This meant her scars would be visible in the short-sleeved uniform. The next time she came to my office, she looked happier. She reported that she loved her job, the people were warm and friendly, and no one had noticed her scars. I said to her, "When you give love, you are beautiful." She began to understand that beauty is deeper than skin, and she learned to love herself, scars and all.

Another example comes from a woman I knew who was dying of a neurological disease. This woman had come to despise her useless body, but she didn't want to die hating what felt like a bowl of Jell-O sitting in her wheelchair. She decided to stop hating and chose love instead. Every day she sat naked in front of a mirror, loving her body inch by inch. The result: she went into complete remission and was *healed of her disease*.

Self-love also means not letting the opinions, preferences, needs, and desires of others dictate your life. It is *your* life to live—your God-given purpose to fulfill. You are the adult and advocate for the child who still lives inside you. Listen to that child—be your own Peter Pan, Wendy, and Tinker Bell all rolled into one. Spend your life doing those things that stir up your imagination, lift your spirits, and leave you inspired to do more.

People with depression suffer hopelessness—trapped in a life that does not nurture who they are. They can hate themselves for living in a state of sadness and emptiness, and they cannot see how or when the conditions that led to their depression will ever change. If you recognize yourself in this situation, don't waste time blaming yourself for having bad feelings. Use them as red flags to guide you away from danger. Thank the feelings for being a part of you. Depression can be a motivator to change your job, walk away from a relationship, or remove yourself from any circumstance that makes you feel trapped or that drains the life from you. Loving yourself means taking those dark moments and turning them into fuel for creativity. Don't try to deny or ignore your depression. Instead say, "Yes, I am feeling this way. How can it redirect me? What is the gift, the wake-up call in it, so I do not have to experience this again?"

In the future, have happy depressions, creative illnesses, brilliant failures, and positive disintegrations. As Bobbie used to say, never consider yourself a failure—you can always serve as a bad example. Drop the choices that held you back. Choose for yourself the relationships, places, activities, and behaviors that make you grateful to be alive.

Remember Peale's story about the man and his machine—think of your mind, body, and soul as God's machine. At least once a day, look into a mirror for several minutes and reject any negative thoughts that arise. Replace the thoughts with love for all parts of yourself. Look into your eyes, say your name, and tell yourself, "I love you and accept you for all that you are." Imagine looking into the mirror one morning and seeing a child of God staring back at you. Just imagine! When it happens—because it will—be assured that you have finally learned to love yourself. God's rhythm and your rhythm are working in nature's perfect harmony.

CREATION

Man creates a heart lung machine,
Does open-heart surgery and says, "That's great"
God creates a tree and sees that it is good

Man creates a dialysis machine and says,
"That's fabulous"

God creates a fish and sees that it is good

Man does transplant surgery and says,
"That's incredible"

God creates a man and doesn't say it is good

The man wounds his finger and covers it
with a Band-Aid

The wound heals

The tree grows

The fish swims

The open-heart patient dies

The dialysis patient dies

The transplant is rejected

What do we say now?

We say creation cannot be matched

So stop trampling upon it

And become a co-creator

Seek Forgiveness

We prayed so that all bitterness could be taken from us and we could start the life for our people again without hatred. We knew out of our own suffering that life cannot begin for the better except by us all forgiving one another. For if one does not forgive, one does not understand; and if one does not understand, one is afraid; and if one is afraid, one hates; and if one hates, one cannot love. And no new beginning on earth is possible without love. . . . The first step towards this love then must be forgiveness.

– **LAURENS VAN DER POST** (1906–1996),
AFRIKANER AUTHOR, HUMANITARIAN, EDUCATOR,
AND CONSERVATIONIST

Van der Post's novel, *A Far Off Place,* involves two white children and their African bushman companions. When the group escape a massacre, they are forced to flee from the enemy, trek across the desert for many months, and report to authorities what had occurred. Although the book is fiction, the characters experience much of what people all over the world, both white and black, have had to face. Their choices are to transform the evil they experienced or perpetrated into forgiveness of the perpetrator, or to hold on to the bitterness, shame, and hate.

Massacres and the hateful events leading up to them have taken place in cultures throughout history on every continent. Each one of them gave humans a chance to learn about love and hate. Just as Nelson Mandela shared in his autobiography and Jewish survivors of the concentration camps teach in schools and synagogues, until people can forgive their captors, they are not free. They hold the keys to their own freedom.

I keep mentioning the connection between thoughts, attitude, and disease. Those who hold on to bitterness or hate give their bodies' immune systems a message to attack itself. The resulting release of stress hormones creates inflammation as a defense. The body literally becomes the battleground, seeing itself as the enemy. Cancer, heart conditions, and autoimmune diseases often result over time, for they all begin with inflammation. Their chance of a healthy, happy life is far less than those who suffered the same experience and, while not forgetting the experience, they did forgive the perpetrators.

Forgiveness does not mean forgetting or saying the act was okay. Remember, we are designed to forgive. Forgetting does not resolve any issues that were painful to us. When you for-*give*, you give yourself a gift, one that you don't *get* by for-*getting*.

Forgiving breaks the bonds that kept you chained to those who hurt you. They may be stuck in their cells of hate, indifference, and fear, but you get to walk away and live in the light and power of God's love. It may take the help of a counselor or spiritual advisor, and sometimes takes many years to achieve, but your act of forgiving literally saves you. The choice is yours.

Most of us have difficulty forgiving ourselves at some time in our lives. Often it is not about doing bad things but about failing in some way to do the right thing—failing to save the sick child, visit the elderly relative, help the friend, or assist a stranger in difficult circumstances. Survivors of disasters can experience great remorse and feel unable to forgive themselves for being alive, because others died. People also do bad things, and when they realize the pain they caused and see the lives they wrecked, they have to face what they did and carry the burden of guilt. Forgiving yourself for your own callous, thoughtless, or even unintentional act can be very difficult indeed.

As van der Post's characters learned, finding a way to forgiveness, whether forgiving ourselves or others, requires that we reach understanding. Until we understand, we are essentially lost and on the wrong path. The early Hebrew word for "sin" is closer in meaning to the English word *err,* and the word for "sinner" means "one who lost the way." When we become aware of our errors, not only can we genuinely repent, but we can also turn to a different path and redirect our lives and actions.

It may be difficult, but when you have hurt someone or done a poor job, say to them as promptly as you can, "I'm sorry." Don't give 900 reasons why it was alright to do it—don't make excuses or blame others. When you ask for forgiveness of your sins or errors, it is important to make amends to the people you have hurt and fix any damage you have done. If you are sincere in your apology, most people will understand, forgive, and heal. They realize you are willing to learn from your mistakes and not blame others. If people don't accept your apology, you can at least feel better for having tried and for making amends where you could.

Forgiveness will not fill you with its peace and love until you understand its effect on others, genuinely repent, and then set things back as right as you can. If we do this, the Creator forgives us as if we had never sinned. Some believe the repentant sinner stands in a place that even the thoroughly righteous cannot, for the penitent's lesson is felt in the heart and learned at the level of the soul. If you are carrying a burden of guilt, I encourage you to write down what you did and share it with a spiritual advisor or trusted elder. If you cannot find such a person, read your confession out loud to God. Even if the repentance and turning is done in private, God knows and will welcome you back.

We are all here to follow a path. The path is about how you contribute love to the world—in a sense, how you imitate God.

Joseph Heller, author of *Catch-22* and other novels, was paralyzed due to a neurological disease. He wrote about the time his friend Mel Brooks came to see him in the hospital. Brooks walked into his room and commanded, "In the name of Jesus, stand and walk." Heller looked at Brooks and retorted, "It didn't work." Brooks shrugged as he said, "It was worth a try."

I wrote to Mel Brooks and told him, "If you had said 'Your sins are forgiven, it would have worked. This is not a mechanical problem but a spiritual one.'"

Mel wrote back, thanking me for straightening out the Jesus talk, and never again would he forget to say "Your sins are forgiven" before doing his regular mumbo jumbo. His letter ended with "Your sins are forgiven. —Mel." Laughter is always a good ending.

If you are harboring the bitter seeds of hate, fear, or resentment from any past hurt, learn from the characters in van der Post's story. Ask God for the bitterness to be removed from your heart and, in its place, plant seeds of *willingness* to forgive. Take the first step toward love. A wonderful freedom and a new start on life are waiting just for you.

FOR GIVE NESS

Forgiveness
A word that speaks of giving
Perhaps that is why it takes a God to forgive
To heal you or others
In one moment
But can you forget?
Not if within you there is a need
God has no needs, so he can forgive
And forget what you remember.
Can we approach the stature of a deity
Have it all within
And forgive for God's sake?

6

EXPLORE THE MYSTERIES

BUT I WOULD LIKE TO KNOW WHAT I
MYSELF CAN KNOW.
I crave to know the meaning of great words;
I ask that LIFE may be defined, and what
Is LOVE. Perchance I, too, can grasp a key
That opens up the door and for myself
Unveil the Mysteries. Or I may hear
A Voice beyond earth's hearing, or see
A PRESENCE which shall REVEAL TO ME!

– **Ernest and Fenwicke Holmes**

Do you ever wonder about the invisible things beyond our understanding? I'm referring to the deeper realities—the questions that have called to mankind since the beginning of life itself. In their epic poem, the Holmes brothers expressed so beautifully their desire to have a conscious connection with the Great Oneness, a union that transcends physical existence and contains all truth, all understanding. It was this basic human need that, despite their scientific education, drove the brothers' curiosity and motivated them to form a spiritual discipline of faith—one based as much on science as on the mysteries.

In past centuries, people who devoted their lives to gaining spiritual knowledge believed that it doesn't just happen; one had to learn how to be conscious in God's presence. Rituals, study, and devotion to a life of humility under God were considered necessary to bringing this about. Today most people are not inclined to join a silent order in a monastery or convent in order to experience this close communication with God. We realize that such strict disciplines aren't essential for achieving a spiritual life. But attitudes of devotion, curiosity, willingness, and humility will prepare the soil of your inner garden, and your *desire* to know and understand God will water it. Desire is a key element to knowing God and opening the door to the mysteries.

The words *mysticism* and *mystery* originally come from the Greek and relate to the closing of the eyes and lips. They are rooted in darkness and silence—the place one must go in order to seek the light and commune with God. Mystics and ministers were those who learned the pathway to God through silence and who often performed miracles of healing.

The word *doctor,* on the other hand, originates from the medieval French verb *docere,* meaning "to teach." *Doctor* was originally the title used for a master teacher, not a medical practitioner. Sadly, modern medicine has become oriented around fixing disease rather than teaching the mystical path—nature's or God's path—for life, health, and healing. When an unexpected cure happens today, doctors speak of spontaneous remission, as if the disease took a break, rather than use the more appropriate term, *self-induced healing.*

Self-induced healing is the "miracle" that happens when the body gets the internal message "I love my life." Our bodies are constantly reading the biological language of our subconscious. Throughout the day and night, we release neurochemicals (from the brain) and hormones (from the body) that act as symbolic messengers, ensuring we respond appropriately to our environment and circumstances, and that keep our automatic systems like breathing and blood pressure working.

Each body chemical has a distinctive molecular structure. It fits like a key into corresponding keyholes (receptors) that are scattered throughout the brain and body. When the key is turned, the receptors respond—in the same way that we read and respond to words such as STOP or GO and symbols like these: ? ! ☺. When we are happy, these chemical "symbols" engage body systems that support our desire to live. But when we are unhappy or stressed for long periods of time, they react differently. Constant stress and unhappiness weaken the immune system by keeping us in a constant fight-or-flight mode rather than the more healthy and happy rest-and-digest. We may only be driving to work, but if our thoughts are fearful and about the demanding day ahead of us, it alerts the brain to release stress hormones, and our body systems respond as they would to fear and danger. Over time, this drains the body of its energy resources and makes us vulnerable to disease and autoimmune conditions.

One of the great mysteries is how certain symbols appear to be universal across all cultures and all times. These often represent the interconnection between life and spirit. One example is the symbol of three entwined circles, which represents the trinity. It speaks of the eternal nature of God-the-One having three distinct aspects: Father, Son, Holy Spirit, or mind, body, and soul. Other doctrines using similar symbolic themes are the pagan star in a circle, the Buddhist mandala, the Native American medicine wheel, the Hindu lotus, and the Chinese yin-yang. Symbols are more powerful than we realize. They replace words with awareness. They connect us directly to a feeling or concept, and they stop the thinking mind from interfering or judging. God's language—the universal language of consciousness—is full of symbolic imagery and color. This language is what we find in our dreams. Dream imagery might show us what is about to come; it might teach us a lesson, give expression to our unexpressed feelings, or provide some kind of direction when we're seeking answers.

Perhaps the biggest mystery of all is what happens to us after we die. One hears of people who have had close calls and crossed the border into that after-death realm only to be brought back to life again. Many of them have reported that they were conscious after the body died and are able to remember in vivid detail their out-of-body—or near-death—experience. This happened to me as a child, and in this section I will share my story of that event.

Another mystery of the ages is about the angels and spiritual guides that appear in our lives. Sometimes they come as a vision or a voice, while at others they invisibly direct circumstances to our benefit. We might see these events as strange coincidences called synchronicity, one of the mysteries experienced by almost everyone but often dismissed or overlooked.

One of my earliest revelations was that mystical experiences are most often found in the silence where we meet God. I learned that when you know God, you know who you are too. Your thoughts change, and you free yourself from the weight of the world. You gain a new kind of happiness; you live with a PRESENCE that reveals itself to you in so many ways, leaving you with a deep sense of oneness and wonder.

So I ask you not to be afraid of closing your eyes and lips, of entering into mysticism and the silent darkness. Embrace your inner journey with the same innocence, curiosity, and passion expressed in the Holmes brothers' poem. Record your experiences in your Bible II, for you will find that you continue to gain knowledge and understanding from them as the years pass.

I encourage you now to put down your cell phone and turn off the television or computer screen. Find a quiet place where you can be undisturbed. Take a deep breath, and exhale while letting all your cares go. Feel the desire inside your heart and soul. Then ask God to reveal the mysteries to you and reunite you with your eternal, enlightened self.

Learn the Language of Your Soul

There is something peculiar, one might even say mysterious, about numbers . . . I have a distinct feeling that Number is a key to the mystery, since it is just as much discovered as it is invented. It is a quantity as well as meaning.

– **CARL GUSTAV JUNG**

As a psychiatrist, Jung had access to hundreds of patients and case histories, including their drawings and accounts of their dreams. He was fascinated by the symbols and numbers that kept appearing, with similar meanings, in both dreams and drawings. He saw dreams and drawings as doors to the subconscious, where imagery and numbers—the language of the soul—communicate with the conscious mind.

I learned to pay attention to my patients' dreams. If a dream suggested—literally or symbolically—that there was a physical issue we weren't aware of, I would perform a biopsy or other test. Invariably the dream would prove to be diagnostically correct.

Paying attention to my own dreams helped me to grow and understand what was going on in my subconscious. I began to wonder at one point in my career if part of the reason I had become a surgeon and started support groups for cancer patients was to ensure that I was the one sitting behind the desk, not in front of it, dealing with—or dying of—the disease. I felt the weight of their pain and fear on my shoulders, which wasn't doing them or me any good. One night I dreamed I was a passenger in the back of a car. We were going up the side of a mountain when suddenly the car veered off the road and plunged down the mountainside. While everyone else was screaming hysterically, I sat quietly. The dream gave me two realizations: I didn't have to be the driver in charge of everything—including the passengers—and fear of death was not an issue for me personally or professionally. I could be sitting with the other passengers and not be part of their fear. As a result of that dream, I moved my office desk against the wall. Without the desk acting as a barrier, I sat *with* my patients, not opposite them. I could now help them to live and heal and not just focus on their disease.

God, guides, and loved ones who've died may also speak to us in our dreams, for when the logical brain is asleep, we are more receptive to hearing them. Months after my father died, I was still wearing black all the time, reminding me that one day I would die too. This wasn't healthy grieving behavior. One night my father appeared in a dream and said he was worried about me. He took me to heaven to show me a Father's Day event. All the fathers were parading and carrying bright candles. He left me standing next to an angel. The angel pointed to one man who was approaching with a dark candle. The angel handed me a match and said, "Go light it."

As I moved forward, I saw that the man was my dad. I said, "Dad, your candle's out. I am here to light it."

Dad said to me, "They keep lighting my candle, but your tears keep putting it out." He wanted me to see he was alright and to not let his death affect my life, because it was making his time in heaven harder to enjoy. This dream inspired *Buddy's Candle*, a book I wrote for grieving children. I stopped wearing black then and began to live in joy for myself and for my father.

Another time, a voice in my dream said, "Your name is Satchidananda." When I woke, it stayed with me, but I had no idea what it meant or who had said it. I was thrilled to learn from an Indian doctor at the hospital that the name means "being, consciousness, and bliss."

And I will never forget the morning I woke from a dream in which the words "The Many Faces of God" were always in front of me. It occurred to me upon waking that we are all the many faces of God.

Our subconscious and spirit guides can communicate with us through symbolic imagery in drawings as well as dreams. Many years ago I took a workshop led by Elisabeth Kübler-Ross to learn about the subconscious knowledge revealed in children's and adults' drawings. After that I always had my patients do drawings, and we interpreted them together. I shared many examples of these in my recent book *The Art of Healing*. I often tell of the mother who came to my office with her daughter, fearing that the girl had a lymphoma, which ran in the family. I asked the child to draw a self-portrait and gave her crayons and paper. On one side of the paper, she drew a picture of herself with swollen glands in her neck, and on the other, she made a drawing of a large cat with big claws filling the page. I said to her mother, "Don't worry; she has cat scratch fever." Ensuing tests revealed this to be true.

Another child, whom I'll call Sarah, was hospitalized with terminal cancer. One day she drew a picture of a purple butterfly and some flowers. When I explained to the mother that purple is a spiritual color and the butterfly represents transformation, she realized her daughter's soul was trying to communicate that Sarah's time here was nearly finished. The mother decided then to take Sarah home. Having learned from Jung the significance of numbers—not just as numerical symbols but also as quantities—I would ask my patients why they drew this many rays of the sun or windows in a house, etc. Sarah did not have a reason for the number of flowers, but we soon learned their significance. She woke up on her mother's birthday and said, "Mom, I'm dying today to free you from all your troubles," and she died later that day. The number of flowers in the drawing equaled the number of days that passed between her doing the drawing and the day of her death.

Whether we're aware of it or not, we all receive communication through symbols, sometimes as a source of comfort or love, others as a nudge to do something. After a loved one dies, people often find "pennies from heaven." Even a scab can be a symbol that holds a message for you. The scab is an amazing survival mechanism we don't have to think about. It stops us from bleeding to death and protects wounds from infection. I love what John Updike wrote in his poem "Ode to Healing": A scab is "a coin / the body has minted, with an invisible motto: / In God we Trust."

The number eight represents beginnings—just as the eighth day starts a new week. But when you turn the number eight onto its side, it becomes a symbol of infinity—no endings. It wasn't planned this way, but it just so happened that the text of this book—*No Endings, Only Beginnings*—fits naturally into eight sections.

So follow Jung's example, and pay attention to symbols, numbers, and images in your dreams. As soon as you awaken, record your dream in a journal kept beside your bed specially for that purpose. Do drawings whenever you have important matters to consider and choices to make. Create a mandala in your garden with stones and flowers and use it to focus your mind when meditating. If you explore the mystery of God's language with an open heart, the messages will comfort you, guide you, and help you to grow in compassion, wisdom, and love.

Welcome Your Angels and Guides

Man was so created by the Lord as to be able
while living in the body
to speak with spirits and angels, as in fact was
done in the most ancient times;
for, being a spirit clothed with a body,
he is one with them.

– **Emanuel Swedenborg** (1688–1772),
Swedish scientist, philosopher, theologian, and mystic

My awareness of angels or guides grew slowly over a lifetime. It wasn't until I reached early middle age that I met my own spiritual guide. I certainly did not believe I had one at the time. My training as a doctor was all about the sciences, not the mysteries. In that sense I have much in common with Swedenborg, who studied science, nature, and biology in the first half of his life. It wasn't until the second half that he turned toward spiritual matters.

Swedenborg was an extraordinary man who crossed the line between life and death on numerous occasions. He wrote volumes on the afterlife as he experienced it—filled with angels, spiritual guides, layers of worlds, and even other beings in the universe. He explained that we are each assigned a lifelong guide and receive help from other guides and angels as we need them.

In my early 40s, I attended a workshop given by Carl Simonton, who introduced me to creative imagery as a tool for doctors to help their cancer patients. I was skeptical about this visualization therapy and did not expect to have anything happen. But during our meditation, we were directed to meet our inner guide. That's when George appeared to me wearing a cap, a big beard, and gown-type garments. He and I had a meaningful conversation related to my life. Afterward, I wondered, *Was George my imagination let loose during the relaxed state?* He had seemed real, but my scientific training made me hesitant to accept the possibility.

Not long after that event, I was giving a lecture at a spiritual center when I suddenly realized I was not using my prepared material. It flowed out of me with no effort, so I just went with it. When I had finished, a woman said, "I have heard you speak before, but this was better than usual." I agreed. The next woman in line handed me a drawing and said, "There was a man standing in front of you for the entire lecture, so I drew his picture for you." It was George. Any doubts I held about having met my spiritual guide disappeared. That picture now hangs in my office.

Two years later, at the same center, I spoke at a funeral. Psychic healer and friend Olga Worrall came up to me after the service and said, "Bernie, are you Jewish?" When I asked if she was confused—we were at a Christian funeral—she answered, "No, there's a Rabbi standing next to you." She then described George in detail, and for the first time, I understood what he was wearing and what it represented. I no longer have to prepare for speaking events because George takes care of what needs to be said. I am merely his instrument.

I have also received messages from patients and friends who died, and when I passed their words on to loved ones, the messages were meaningful and accurate. As Swedenborg states, I am a spiritual being with a body clothing it; because God and creation use the language of consciousness, my spirit understands when another spirit speaks to me. Remember, we can all be used as one of God's angels or his God-on-Duty in disguise.

Sometimes our loved ones who have died act as angels for us, giving us loving messages, comforting us in difficult times, or providing protection when we're in danger. When my co-author, Cynthia, was hospitalized with a serious viral infection at age 15, she had an encounter with just such an angel:

I was so ill and in such pain, all I wanted to do was join my mother, who had died three years before. After I'd been in the hospital for a week with no sign of improvement, everyone—including the doctors—grew worried, for they were running out of options. Then something extraordinary happened.

The plain wall at the foot of my bed just opened up, and I found myself standing on a hillside covered with tall grasses and beautiful wild flowers. My dearest friend, Shep—our old border collie who had died the year after Mom's death—suddenly appeared from over the horizon. She bounded into the meadow, black fur shining, eyes sparkling, and she was young again. We played together, chasing, leaping, dancing, and rolling down the hill, deliriously happy to be reunited. I could feel my depleted spirit and body literally filling up with the warmth of Shep's love for me and her enthusiasm for life. Then, as suddenly as she had appeared, Shep ran over the crest of the hill and was gone. I called to her, but the meadow faded away, and I found myself in bed once again, staring at the hospital wall.

A few moments later, the doctor and nurses came into my room. I excitedly told them about my dead dog's visit and that it wasn't a dream. They said I must have been hallucinating because of the high fever, but when they

> took my temperature, they found the fever had gone. I then sat up, hungry and eager to eat for the first time in over a week. I made a complete turnaround and was released from the hospital a few days later.
>
> Even today, in my 60s, I know the vision was not a result of wishful thinking or imagination. I had wanted to die. Shep came to me—totally unexpected. I lived it, felt it, heard it, and saw it. She wanted me to live, to enjoy life to the fullest, and to know that I was loved—no matter what. She came as my healing angel, and it worked!

Cynthia's story touched my heart, for we both have deep bonds with our animals—whether they're in the body or in spirit. If you seek and have a vision, or an angel comes of its own accord, don't say it can't be real. Accept it as reality—as your teacher. A true vision or visitation will stay with you for life, and the understandings it brings will expand over time.

In the stillness of meditation, thank your angels for their service and love. Invite your spiritual guide to introduce himelf or herself. When they appear, welcome them with love. Practice being still at least once every day to remember your true nature—for you are spirit and are one with them. Let the mystery become your reality.

See Synchronicity in Action

Meaningful coincidences are thinkable as pure chance. But the more they multiply and the greater and more exact the correspondence is, the more their probability sinks and their unthinkability increases, until they can no longer be regarded as pure chance but, for lack of a causal explanation, have to be thought of as meaningful arrangements. . . . Their "inexplicability" is not due to the fact that the cause is unknown, but to the fact that a cause is not even thinkable in intellectual terms.

– **Carl Gustav Jung**

Physicists now accept that consciousness is non-local—that there is a unity between all atoms and molecules, all life, and everything in existence. On some level they can and do communicate and take action at the same time or in perfect sequence, regardless of any distance between them. This is not a new concept. Jung saw so much evidence of this in his own life and in the lives of others that he wrote about it in his essays, calling it "synchronicity" and "meaningful coincidence."

When opportunities assemble and align themselves as if someone or something had placed all the people, things, and circumstances into the flawless order of heaven, the right things happen at just the right times. This is synchronicity. When we embrace our purpose at a deep level, love those whom we serve, and love what we do, we are in harmony with God. Our love and purpose merge into that oneness, create a positive force, and miracles or meaningful coincidences begin to happen—big ones and little ones.

A series of such events happened to me when I was ready to enter medical school. I had applied to the University of Michigan and requested that they accept me early into their program in order to forestall my being drafted. This way I could finish medical school before serving in the Army and then, when I did enlist, I would serve as a physician. It wasn't a straightforward task for the admissions team, as extra forms needed to be filled out and permissions sought from the right departments. But in the end they agreed, and I was accepted into their school. At the same time, Dr. Foster, my advisor and head of the Zoology Department at Colgate, wanted me to select Cornell Medical College, based upon my personality and how hard I worked. He advised that it would be better for me to attend a school that didn't give out grades, for he knew I drove myself hard enough. Then another situation arose.

That summer I met Bobbie. We were both counselors at Robin Hill Day Camp in Yonkers, New York—she for the first-grade girls and I for the boys. When we first met, I had an immediate sense of a path—the feeling of a blueprint already laid out before the two of us. Because of this extraordinary connection with her, I decided I didn't want to go to the University of Michigan after all. I wanted to stay closer to New York, where Bobbie was going to be teaching, so we could maintain our relationship.

I wrote to Michigan, afraid that they would be upset with me for turning them down, especially after they had gone out of their way to take me early. I explained that I had met a young woman and didn't want to go all the way to Michigan, where I'd be so far from her. I received such a wonderful letter from the dean; I wish now I had saved it. He said Michigan was such a fine school, he couldn't understand why I'd want to go anywhere else, except for a reason such as love. Because of this, and that I hadn't downgraded my opinion of the medical school, he could accept my wish and grant it with no ill feelings. Everything then worked out as smoothly, as if it had been planned that way all along, including my admittance to Cornell Medical College in New York City.

When I arrived at Cornell, I was assigned to a double room in the nurse's dormitory. My roommate learned that a friend of his was also coming to Cornell and asked if I would switch rooms. I did, despite the fact that I was leaving a room in the nurse's dormitory—which my father thought was a nice place to be, surrounded by all the female nursing students—for a room in an old Army barracks across the street from the school. But there are no coincidences!

My new roommate was Fred Smith, an engineer in his mid-30s who had decided to change his career and go to medical school. I was 20 at the time, while Fred was 36, so Fred became like a father figure to me. I realize now what a benefit that was. He kept me calm and seated at my desk in our room, disengaged from all the other students who were frantically running around, worrying about what they knew or did not know or what grade they would get on a test.

After my first year of medical school, Bobbie and I were married and moved into a small apartment. I took the subway to school every morning, about an hour's ride. Once again, I was separated from the unhealthy environment of the medical school. By unhealthy, I mean the stress on facts, the absence of feeling, and the focus on grades and disease rather than on the people. This feeds into all the hysteria that manifests in such a cloistered situation and insulated environment. I was out in the world, realizing life has other challenges and issues besides medical school exams. Yes, I studied and worked hard, but there was a balance in my life that was much healthier than circumstances in the dormitory. In my lap and lying on the pages of my textbooks were our two cats—rescued by Bobbie from outside her classroom.

With such a loving, balanced environment to study in, I did very well. I was Phi Beta Kappa in college, and in medical school I achieved membership in the honor society Alpha Omega Alpha. This placed me academically in the top five or six of the class. Because the school only told you your grades if you were in the lowest quarter of the class, I was surprised by my results. I had been doing the best I could with my studies, not competing with anyone but myself, and I remained focused on helping people because that made me happy. That's why I had chosen to be a doctor in the first place.

When you act from the heart in an egoless way and love unconditionally, it changes your life. All the things we touch in nature and all our acts change the world. When you are unattached to the results but simply involved in the act of living, everyone benefits. Everything falls miraculously into place.

Synchronicity continued to happen for me. I was in training for pediatric surgery in Pittsburg when I developed severe pain and swelling in the joints of my fingers, which made it difficult to operate. I was diagnosed with arthritis. I feared all my training was now without purpose, but at the same time, I reached out to the Army, where I learned that this meant I would be unable to enter active military duty. The Army didn't want a disabled surgeon. But here's the miracle part of the story: when we returned to Connecticut, the pain and swelling disappeared, and the disease never returned.

When you devote yourself to helping others in a way that you are passionate about, you will be amazed how God's love activates in your life. Recognize synchronicity when it happens. Have you experienced a series of coincidences? List them in your journal and keep adding them as they happen. Realize each time God is patting you on the back, saying, "Well done."

Reflect upon Near-Death Experiences

To know that we maintain an identity independent of the physical body is proof enough of immortality.

– **Ernest Holmes**

This statement was first proven for me when I was a child. How? I left my body and—fully conscious and aware of myself as myself—I experienced the other side of life. I experienced death. I have shared parts of this story before, but it bears retelling in more detail, for the experience shaped my whole life.

When I was four, I was sick in bed with an ear infection. I was playing with a toy telephone, pulling the parts off and putting them on again. I was mimicking the carpenters I'd seen who put nails in their mouths to free their hands and would take the nails out as they needed them. With so many parts in my mouth, I aspirated the screws and dial, and they became lodged in my throat. My larynx shut down in a complete spasm, leaving me unable to breathe, cry for help, or make a sound.

I separated from the boy on the bed and observed his body desperately trying to suck in air. The convulsive efforts of his chest and diaphragm were caused by an uncontrollable reflex response, a struggle that looked incredibly painful. Yet here I was, totally at peace, free of all pain, knowing I was dying and that nothing was wrong with the fact that I was dying. The thought lingered that my mother would be very sad and angry because a good child just didn't do something like this. But I felt it was alright to go, because the boy on the bed was struggling and I wasn't. I knew the dying body on the bed was not me and that my spirit and consciousness were very much alive. Death was not something to be afraid of. No words can explain it adequately, but I felt perfect, in a state of pure bliss and unconditional love.

Then, from out of nowhere, a forceful effort expelled air from the boy's lungs, as if someone had performed a Heimlich maneuver. The boy on the bed vomited, making all the toy parts shoot out. I was now back in my body and could breathe again. Having heard me vomiting, my mother rushed into my room. My first spoken words were, "Who did that?" I had chosen death, but someone had interfered. I was upset and angry when "sucked" back into my body. But I had a real sense of someone else deciding I wasn't supposed to die at that moment. Even as a four-year-old, I thought of God.

Though I didn't have the words to express it at the time, the whole event brought me to the realization that I am not just a physical body but also spirit, soul, and consciousness. I also understood my time wasn't up, which meant I had some purpose to fulfill. It was my first inkling that living in the body happened so that my soul could learn. This sense stayed with me my entire life, though not always consciously. Becoming aware of what path I was meant to take happened over time.

It wasn't until I was a doctor with a crazy, busy schedule that I came to understand we enter the physical realm for more than one lifetime. A friend who knew the inner struggle I was going through at the time asked me over the phone, "Why are you living this life?" Immediately I fell into a sort of trance and saw myself as a knight whose liege was wealthy and powerful. My lord ordered me to kill the daughter of his enemy, which I did with my sword, and I killed her dog at the same time. I recognized my wife in this lifetime as my victim. I realized later that our marriage in this life helped in uniting our families and resolved the horrible acts of the past while teaching us to have faith in our true Lord. Other past life experiences revealed that Bobbie and

I had shared several lives, playing different character roles with lessons to learn in each one.

With the first one, a realization came to me that being a surgeon in this life may be my way of helping people with a knife rather than killing with the sword. My lifelong habit of rescuing animals also relates to the life of the sword-wielding knight. When our kids were little, I used to read to them one of their favorite stories about a knight who returned from war only to find his baby's blood-spattered crib overturned and his bloody dog beside it. Thinking the dog must have killed his child, the knight killed the dog, but when he righted the crib, he found his baby sleeping—unharmed and alive—next to a dead wolf. The faithful dog had protected the child and killed the wolf, and now the dog was dead by the hand of his own master. This part of the story always made me cry, and my children would comfort me, saying, "It's just a story, Dad; you don't have to cry." I realize now that it connected me with the sorrow my soul still feels for my actions in the past life.

My soul has learned many lessons over countless lifetimes, lessons it could not have learned without entering the physical world. Having come to know this, to see it for myself, confirms to me that life is never-ending. You and I *are* immortal.

When we leave our bodies, time no longer exists. The next time you see a five-year-old playing a violin in a concert orchestra, you can be certain he or she has been here before, mastering that same instrument.

Each time our spirits enter a new body, we pass through a sort of filter, leaving memories of our previous lives and the majority of our souls' senses and understandings behind. We must enter the darkness of ignorance each time we are born and begin to seek the light to find our pathway back to the Creator, just as God created light out of the darkness in order to understand creation. Once you truly understand our eternal nature, you have no more fear of death.

Everyone could use a near-death experience. When we see for ourselves what a gift each life is, we no longer wish to waste time and energy on those thoughts, desires, and actions that have no meaning. But the majority of people have yet to experience full consciousness of what they are. For those who haven't, there are many inspiring accounts of near-death and past life experiences in books and videos. I encourage you to read some of these books and watch the videos. Keep an open mind if you wish to grasp that we are all here doing God's work, becoming godlike in this life through the lessons we learn in the physical world. It is as natural as the rain falling, if only we remain open to it. Put away the umbrella of intellect, and let the spiritual bathe you. Let it wash away the barriers so you can become aware of the oneness and unifying order of life.

Don't wait for death or a near-death experience to awaken you to the voice and reality of God's love. Have a near-life experience, and connect with the never-ending, always-beginning consciousness of your true being, your Highest Self.

7

SHARE YOUR STORIES

The new discoveries of science "rejoin us to the ancients" by enabling us to recognize in this whole universe "a reflection magnified of our own most inward nature; so that we are indeed its ears, its eyes, its thinking, and its speech—or, in theological terms, God's ears, God's eyes, God's thinking, and God's word."

–**Bill Moyers**, quoting **Joseph Campbell** (1904–1987), American professor of literature and comparative mythology

Campbell found, in the study of mythology, that stories—whether real or mythological—impart deep truths, giving us a sense of our immortality and God's eternity. Long before people became literate, stories and songs were used to pass important memories, skills, and knowledge from one generation to another. Stories knitted families and communities together, maintained cultural identity, and helped people to survive in their environment.

Campbell understood that we are all one family, one creation. New discoveries in science and physics are bringing us closer to the ancients—our ancestors—whether the discoveries involve DNA and memory or the phenomenon of nonlocality, which illustrates that time, place, and distance are man-made theories and that nothing truly separates us. The more we learn about how we are connected to past, present, and future, and across great expanses, the closer we come to understanding our true nature, our familial connection with God. Two of my favorite books exploring this area are *The Science of Mind* by Ernest Holmes and *The Science of God* by Gerald L. Schroeder, Ph.D.

People with no family stories or culture to fall back on can sometimes feel disconnected from the past. Their innate habits and preferences have no apparent origin and lack meaning. Life just starts and stops in each generation. But electronically available archives, often going back hundreds of years, now make it easy to research families online. When we discover our own ancestors' stories, even the ones we never knew existed, it brings us emotionally closer to them in a very real sense. As we recognize similar traits, core values, and motivations between this generation and those who lived before, we gain new insight about ourselves and current family members. If you've never done any family research, why not give it try? You'll be surprised what you discover.

Most people don't realize that our significant feelings and experiences are stored in the tissues of the body and in our genes. Major events of the past are still residing in us, changing us, and leading to psychological and physical health—or illness—depending on how those events affected us and what we did with them. A grandmother who suffered starvation in childhood may affect, through her genes, how her grandchildren's bodies metabolize fats, while her anxiety over food and having enough to live on may also be passed down, even if the children never get to meet her. Both psyche and matter are the issue. Mind is not just in the brain; it is in the cells of our bodies and even the ether of the universe.

I was introduced to this phenomenon of nonlocality when I talked to patients who had received organ transplants. A proportion of those who received major organs like hearts, lungs, or kidneys have reported being aware that the organs in their bodies originated from someone quite different from them. They suddenly knew certain facts previously unknown, felt unfamiliar feelings, and had different preferences as soon as they awakened from surgery.

A friend of mine, Claire Sylvia, had a heart-lung transplant and wrote a book about her experience, *A Change of Heart*. After her transplant surgery, she had cravings for things she'd never enjoyed, like beer and Chicken McNuggets. She also experienced a strong desire to ride a motorcycle, but she had never liked motorbikes. Later she had a dream in which a young man told her his name was Tim L. She eventually found an obituary for a man named Tim, his last name beginning with L. He had been 18 years old when he died in a motorcycle accident just before her surgery. Claire contacted the family, and it turned out that yes, Tim was her donor, and all the cravings she had been experiencing were for *his* favorite things.

How do the knowledge and preferences of one person enter the consciousness of another if thoughts and feelings only live in the physical brain? Even if Tim's organs were able to biologically inform Claire's body about his preferences, it doesn't explain how he entered her dream and gave her his name and other facts. We must not deny this soul connection exists just because we don't have the answer.

As Campbell says, every person is a living reflection of the same thing—our inward nature—which is God's nature. In a real sense we carry God in all our experiences and all our stories. Just think about that for a moment. Through us, God has become the greatest storyteller of all.

In this section, I share some family stories that shaped me and my children—events that, in hindsight, became valuable sources of wisdom. I hope you will recognize and appreciate the things that we all share, that make us all family. Add your family stories to your own Bible II or life manual. Each time you revisit them, they will appear both familiar and fresh. Your "most inward nature" will be magnified by them, and life's lessons will become more deeply ingrained in the psyche and matter of you.

Honor Your Parents and Grandparents

Try to remember that a good man can never die. You will see him many times. You will see him in the streets. You will see him in the houses, in all the places of the town. . . . You will feel him in all things that make this a world for us to live in. You will feel him in all things that are here out of love, and for love—all the things that are abundant, all the things that grow. The person of a man may leave—or be taken away—but the best part of a good man stays. It stays forever. Love is immortal and makes all things immortal. But hate dies every minute.

– **William Saroyan**

Saroyan's quote always reminds me of my parents and grandparents. Their legacy was one of love, and it is a legacy that just keeps growing. I can see them in what we did with our lives and also in the actions of our children and grandchildren. Of course, our parents and grandparents made mistakes and did things that perhaps they wish they hadn't, but the best part of them has stayed and will keep staying as long as kindness, faith, humor, and loving exist. My parents, Si and Rose, and Bobbie's parents, Ado and Merle, played supportive roles after Bobbie and I were married, and they stayed active in our kids' lives as they were growing up.

Before she had me, my mother was extremely debilitated by weight loss and weakness due to a severe case of hyperthyroidism. She was told not to have children, for the added stress of a pregnancy could be life-endangering. But her mother wanted a grandchild, and she forced food into my mother until she gained weight and went on to conceive. The pregnancy was complicated, and when my mother was way past her due date, she endured more than a week of labor. Finally, the doctor performed a high forceps delivery, explaining my mother would not survive a cesarean section.

It wasn't until my adult years that Mom told me she was handed not an infant but a "purple melon." She described my head as being "like a cucumber." In either event, I wasn't terribly attractive. After taking me home from the hospital, she wrapped me in sheets and hid me from onlookers in a covered carriage behind the house. My appearance was something she found embarrassing to deal with, especially when neighbors came to see the new baby. Until Mom explained this to me, I had always wondered why the family album only contained photos of a covered baby carriage and none of me as a newborn.

My grandmother, who had raised six children, was less threatened by my appearance. She stepped in and, several times a day, would anoint my head with oil and massage it. She gently worked her hands over my features and the swollen parts and pushed things back where they belonged. So I was an ugly duckling with a different story. I wasn't thrown out of the nest feeling rejected, unloved, and struggling to see my beauty. I was loved, accepted, and protected from critical eyes. I am sure I felt more like a swan than an ugly duckling.

I don't know what would have happened to me if not for my grandmother's intervention. Development of the immune system and various organs, including the brain, will not happen if babies aren't touched and held. The distinguished anthropologist Dr. Ashley Montagu wrote in his 1971 book *Touching: The Human Significance of the Skin* that the death rate for infants under a year old was nearly 100 percent in numerous U.S. orphanages from the 1850s to 1920. In those orphanages, babies were not touched, for fear of spreading infection, but most of them died of infections anyway. Without physical nurturing, their immune function and development were nonexistent.

When my mother's hyperthyroidism went away after my birth, I am sure she saw me as a gift or miracle, and again, I felt loved. I know now that it was not miraculous but biological, as fetal stem cells can often provide the mother with what is needed to repair her injured body.

I know that the memory of our lives is stored in our bodies, and I am sure that is one of the reasons I have a shaved head today. Fifty years after my birth, I was massaged by a woman therapist for the first time. When her hands massaged my head, it was an incredible experience. After several minutes I opened my eyes and found the room filled with people. When I asked why they were all there, the chief massage therapist said, "We thought you had a heart attack or a stroke. You were gone. We couldn't communicate with you." I then told him about my birth and the body memories the other therapist's hands had brought back for me. I had retreated into that infant state of speechless, wordless bliss under my grandmother's fingers.

I often ask people, "What things do you remember your parents saying that have helped you survive or have worked to destroy you?" In the case of my parents, I think all the messages I heard and remember were ones that made a positive difference, for they were messages of love. I was lucky because I always felt certain that both of my parents loved me. I also overheard my dad saying nice things about me when I wasn't in the room. It made me feel what he was saying was the truth and not just said to please me. Do this for your kids and family; it's an incredibly powerful gift.

My grandfather died of tuberculosis, leaving his wife and six children with nothing when my father was only 12. Dad told me once it was one of the best things that ever happened to him. Shocked, I asked him what he was talking about, and he said, "It taught me what was important about life." My dad was mature enough and wise enough to learn from it. For him material things are for improving everyone's life, not just your own. He always spent time and money helping others and teaching me lessons. For his entire life, he tried to make life easier for everyone he met. His philosophy was passed on to his children, for kids copy what they see and experience.

A good example of Dad's parenting style happened when I was a youngster. I broke my neighbor's toy as we were playing with it in the yard. I felt jealous over what he had and I didn't. The boy's family told my folks, but I wasn't punished. The next day Dad came home from work with the same toy. He handed it to me and said, "I know you wanted one of these," and then he just walked into the house. I could have kept it for myself, and he wouldn't have said anything, but I knew he would be disappointed in me. I loved my father so much I never wanted to upset him. By giving me the toy, he was showing he trusted me to do the right thing. He didn't embarrass me and take it to the neighbor himself. That's the kind of guy he was. Dad taught us to follow our hearts and let our hearts make up our minds. I took the toy over to my friend's house and gave it to him. After that, I felt like I had taken a test and gotten an A+. Dad's loving discipline reinforced our values of honesty and kindness while it increased our sense of self-respect. Let this story help you to invest your children with positive messages rather than negative judgments or shaming punishments.

I often think of my mother's advice, "Do what will make you happy." My parents didn't always agree with choices I wanted to make, but they lived by their motto and loved me enough to respect my choices. My father was the financial vice president at American Broadcasting-Paramount Theatres. He had hoped to help me enter his line of work, but I decided to study medicine. He didn't get upset or pressure me to change. And when I felt guilty about asking him for financial help to go to med school, get married, and rent an apartment, he told me, "If I don't want to help you, I'll say no." He was teaching me survival behavior way back then. *Just as you should do what makes you happy, you should also say no to what doesn't.* Write that quote in your Bible II. It's a good one.

My mother taught me that missed opportunities are not disasters. She'd say, "God is redirecting you." Her attitude was all about being grateful for spiritual flat tires. The spiritual flat tire is the one that occurs on the way to the airport, making you miss your plane. You feel upset about it until you learn that the plane you missed crashed after takeoff. Thank God for the flat tire and for the love and guidance of parents and grandparents.

If you remember your parents' mottoes—the phrases they always said—write them down. Think about how they improved your life and the lives of others. If you only received unloving messages from your parents, let those sayings die. Think instead of the people who played a loving role for you—who did and said things to inspire you. Write down their sayings. If you can't think of anyone, you can re-parent yourself and make up your own sayings based on what you would say to a child you dearly love. Be the immortal "best part" of you that passes from one generation to another. Let the hate die as you spread the love that goes on forever. Every time you do, you heal the world.

Make Marriage Your Heaven

But each absorbed in each, and each in one,
Through love are merged, and life in heav'n begun.

– **Ernest and Fenwicke Holmes**

Like the Holmes brothers, I think of marriage as a third entity created by the love of two separate people. It doesn't mean one person in the marriage has to change and become like the other; it means that *the union itself* becomes an entity, a living thing. It needs to be fed, nurtured, enjoyed, respected, protected, and upheld by both partners, despite all the things that life and the world throw at it.

When parents share with their kids heartwarming and funny stories about their relationship, it helps the next generation to see how healthy relationships develop and to enjoy what marriage can bring. They feel supported and encouraged by hearing about the times Mom and Dad were acting crazy but could still have a good laugh about it afterward. It's often the little everyday things that teach so much.

For example, Bobbie didn't like my method of filling the dishwasher. I do it like a surgeon, putting everything close together, not leaving any space around the objects inside. One day an exasperated

Bobbie showed me 11 cups, all of them with their handles broken off. Having proven her point about how to fill the machine, Bobbie then wanted me to throw the cups out, but I felt they were still useful, despite the fact they didn't have handles. I put the cups in a bag and, without telling Bobbie, took them to our vacation house in Cape Cod. The next time we went there to relax for a few days, I knew she would see them first thing in the morning, so I went jogging before she got up.

I always carry a little plastic bag to pick up litter and recyclable items when I'm jogging, and this day was no exception. I was running along a main road when there in front of me, sitting on the yellow divider strip, was a white cup with a broken handle. I felt God had something to do with this; she knew about my guilty conscience over those 11 cups back at the house. I ran over to the cup, picked it up, and turned it over. Printed on it was a picture of two elephants hugging, with the words "I love you just the way you are." I laughed then, for I knew this was God's message to all of us. I put the cup in my bag and took it home, knowing when Bobbie saw it she would accept all the other broken cups. By the way, decades later, it is still sitting in our home on the kitchen table.

I got to know Bobbie in the summer we both worked as camp counselors in upstate New York. At first I was attracted to her beauty, but her sweet nature and great sense of humor just bowled me over. She had many boyfriends, and one of the fraternities declared her the most attractive girl at her college, so I never expected her to go out with me, and I never asked. One day while we were watching the camp kids at the poolside, I said it was nice that they kept the pool open at night for use by the counselors.

She looked at me and said, "Are you asking me for a date?"

I wasn't, but I jumped in with a yes, and she said okay. Now, Bobbie was never on time in her entire life. The pool had closed by the time she appeared, ready to go swimming, so we went to a local pub instead and talked for a couple of hours. From that night on, our friendship grew into love, and our love for each other never ended. Through all the years we had together, I really felt like we were one person; we were complete and needed nothing more in order to be happy.

One of the things that attracted me to Bobbie was that she loved cats and all animals. She used to feed the feral cats who sat outside her classroom when she taught grade school. She never stopped bringing them home from school, and even after the kids were born, she took in stray and rescued animals of all kinds. We were both happy to make them part of our family. Eventually we had five children plus a whole zoo of creatures, indoors and out. This is discussed in my book *Love, Animals & Miracles*, but I can tell you, after a day in the OR, it was stressful for me to come home and deal with sick or wounded animals or perform an emergency cesarean section for a hamster on the kitchen table.

I'm sorry to say I didn't always have a good attitude about the pandemonium at the Siegel house and zoo. One day our son Jeff asked me, "Are you and Mom getting a divorce?"

"Why are you asking that?"

"Because you yell a lot."

"What makes you think yelling means we are getting a divorce?"

"My friend's parents yell, and they are getting a divorce."

"Jeff, I just yell when I am angry and when I don't like what is happening related to your behavior." He stood there thinking about what I had said, so I stopped what I was doing and gave him a hug. "We are not getting a divorce. I love your Mom," I assured him, and out the door he went to play.

I have learned to apologize for not knowing how to be a better husband, father, or doctor. I can't fix everything. I listen to the people who depend on me in these different roles when they express their feelings and needs, and I change my attitude and behavior when I'm in the wrong. That is what counts—not excuses or perfection but love and compassionate caring. So ask your loved ones to speak to you and not be afraid of letting you know when you need to act better. It lets them know you care. If you can listen and not make excuses; laugh with each other; share, or at least appreciate, the same values; and have love and respect for each other, you can get through anything.

When the Holmes brothers wrote, "each absorbed in each," I believe they meant when each person is fully invested in the emotional experience of the other. Total empathy. In other words, their partners' emotional well-being is *as important as their own.* There will be differences of opinion and preferences in every marriage, but these do not become insurmountable problems if the most important thing between the individuals is their bond, their being together. No preference, no opinion will take priority over this. Mutually invested love makes the marriage a harbor, a home, and a living heaven.

Raise Your Children with Humor

Sufficient unto the day is one baby. As long as you are in your right mind don't you ever pray for twins. Twins amount to a permanent riot. And there ain't any real difference between triplets and an insurrection.

– **Mark Twain** (1835–1910),
American writer, publisher, lecturer, and humorist

Being a father of twins, this quote always makes me laugh, for you've got to have a sense of humor if you want to survive being a parent. Raising children is probably the hardest yet most important and rewarding responsibility you will ever have.

When you're exasperated with the kid who stuffed his socks down the toilet just to see what would happen after he flushed, it is important to remember that one day, he will be an adult and will remember if you treated him with understanding and compassion or lost your sense of humor and made him feel bad about himself for being curious.

Bobbie and I became engaged during my first year in medical school and were married at the end of the year. When we settled in New Haven for my internship and residency, Bobbie was already pregnant.

We felt, now that we were done with school, we could start our family. I really wanted kids and was thrilled to be on the way to fatherhood. Back then it was against policy to allow fathers in the delivery room, but I had just started to work in the hospital, and people thought I was with our obstetrician. So I watched Jonathan's birth. It was an incredible feeling you just can't put into words. To hold my newborn child was like holding a miracle.

Several days after we brought Jon home, Bobbie had a hemorrhage and, after the police didn't respond to my call, I took her back to the emergency room myself. It was Sunday, and I was scheduled to make rounds with the staff and chief of surgery. I told him where Bobbie was and expected him to say, "Go to the ER and be with your wife," but he didn't. I had to stay and do my part, giving each patient's history to the team.

Jonathan did not know who I was because our schedules didn't coincide. When I was home, he was usually sleeping, and when I was sleeping or at the hospital, he was awake. The first time he was left at home with me, he screamed because he didn't know who this strange man was, and the neighbors had to come over to calm him. I think they felt worse than I did. So when you go into the hospital, remember that doctors and nurses are people too. They need your understanding and compassion just as much as you need theirs.

Over the next seven years, Jeffrey, Stephen, and the twins—Carolyn and Keith—were born. Others seem to think we had it easy in our marriage and parenting, but we had our challenges, just like any other family. Bobbie and I were tired and busy finishing training, moving, caring for the children, and starting practice. Adding to those challenges was another more serious one—the twins had been born with a hearing impairment due to Bobbie's exposure to German measles from one of our babysitters. This hearing impairment, plus nervous system and immune system problems, manifested itself due to the effects of the measles virus upon their developing fetuses.

After our first three boys, I very much wanted a daughter. When the twins arrived, Carolyn was born first, and her brother Keith was our bonus. Bobbie's sense of humor always helped sustain me. When she learned she was carrying twins, she said to me, "If it's two more boys, I am not coming home from the hospital." It was a relief then to hear the obstetrician say, "What a gentleman, letting your sister out first."

We found it both upsetting and interesting to see how medical professionals and teachers responded to the twins' undiagnosed hearing impairment.

They were constantly criticized and blamed for their behavior. Bobbie talked to the pediatrician about Keith's behavior at home and school, and rather than looking further into the problem, the doctor said, "He's just distracted, thinking of other things." The nursery school, which specialized in child development and was staffed by supposedly skilled personnel, never suggested that perhaps Keith and Carolyn weren't hearing them. Instead the teachers complained that the twins didn't pay attention and were disruptive. It took Bobbie's insistence to have the children tested and the hearing impairment verified. Keith was tested first because he acted out more. Carolyn was more ladylike, and a year later she was tested and also found to be hearing-impaired.

Our children have always let me know when I am not "acting like a father." When they were kids, they'd say "Dad, you're not in the operating room now" when I was taking charge or giving orders—something that you might have to do in the operating room as the responsible person or captain of the ship. At home, they were not my staff or assistants, they were my family, and they let me know it. If emotional issues came up, the children would tell me if I wasn't handling it well.

We also shared a lot of laughter, and this strengthened our family bonds. When my sons were suggesting titles for one of my books, *Out of My Mind* was mild compared to some others that I hesitate to document. Sharing a sense of humor with your kids means they get a chance to roast you on occasion, and you can laugh at it. One such comment came when I was to be given an award by Unity Church at their annual meeting. This award was given to many prestigious individuals over the years. I said I would be happy to come and be a speaker, but I didn't believe I fit into a league with Mother Teresa or Norman Vincent Peale. They replied, "No, you have helped many people, and we want to give you this award," so I accepted. When I came home to tell our children that I was going to receive this award, Jonathan said, "I guess they must have lowered their standards." This jesting, I believe, is healthy and good for ego control. I also knew how to get even. I would ask, "Do you know why your mother and I will never get a divorce? Because neither one of us wants the children!" Again, the kids knew it was said in jest, and we all laughed together. They knew they were loved by how we treated them.

We always tried to support the kids' interests. They each raised different kinds of creatures; some had snakes, rodents, lizards, or insects, while others had guinea pigs, goats, ducks, and so on. Our son Stephen, who had an early interest that overlapped with my own, would often accompany me to the hospital, for he was stimulated by the activity there. Many times I would have surgery scheduled and couldn't be with him, so I let him wear a scrub suit and wait in the receiving and holding area for the OR. He came to know his way around the hospital and became a junior orderly, known to the staff.

One day the chief of surgery called me and said it was inappropriate for a child to be in the operating room. I said to him, "Come and watch him with me for a minute." Stephen, in a scrub suit, greeted new and anxious patients and gave their charts to the nurse. It startled them to see a child taking their chart, but then they relaxed and smiled, realizing he was not going to be their surgeon. They actually felt comforted and amused by his presence. His head barely came up to the height of the stretcher they were on. After that, nothing more was ever said about bringing Stephen to work. He continued running around, doing errands, and just being there for people. The effect of that humanity is something I began to understand—the childlike innocence and trust and the healing it created. We need not only an intensive care unit but also an intensive caring unit in our hospitals. We didn't have high-risk patients; we had high-hope patients.

One day some of our children were battling with each other as they were leaving for school, and I said, "Why don't you just say, 'I'm sorry. I love you.'" They turned to me, very hurt, and said, "You're sorry you love us?" I said, "No, I am sorry, period. I love you, period." They missed my punctuation and got the wrong message. We laughed, and love returned. Another time when they were arguing, I said, "You may choose peace or conflict." Our daughter, Carolyn, announced, "I'll have pizza!" Argument ended, and laughter filled the room.

I'm so grateful that our children grew into heart-based, compassionate adults and went on to become wonderful parents. If there is ever a reward beyond all others, it is receiving your adult children's "thank you" for making them feel loved and watching them pass that love on to your grandchildren. Even after Bobbie's passing, I still see her in the kids and hear her laughter in theirs. The trials we endured, the lessons we learned, the fun we all had together—and still have—fill me with nothing but joy.

Make sure to set aside plenty of time to have fun with your kids and not spend all your days transporting them from here to there and doing the necessary chores. Listen to your kids when they tell you they're not happy with how you are treating them and change your approach. Lighten up and just love them. And when the noise level in the house rises from "riot" to "insurrection," remember to keep your funny bone in good condition and use it often. All too soon they'll be grown and gone. I hope one day when they are adults, your kids will look you in the eyes and say, "Thanks, Mom. Thanks, Dad. You were the best."

8

UNDERSTAND THAT ENDINGS ARE ALWAYS BEGINNINGS

When you reach the end of what you should know, you will be at the beginning of what you should sense.

– **Kahlil Gibran** (1883–1931),
Lebanese-American writer, poet, and visual artist

I see life as a series of beginnings. Each day we awaken to the sum total of what we've lived and experienced so far, or as Gibran puts it, "the end of what we should know." And we enter each day with our intuition and heart—what we "should sense." Gibran was a great seeker of truth—a mystic—a deeply spiritual, curious, and expressive man who lived through his heart and creative soul.

I believe he understood that we must look at what we are creating *in this present moment* because we never know which moment is our last. Ideally we would think, act, and live every moment as our last one. But we are, after all, spiritual beings having a *human* experience, and we are designed to forget so that we will make mistakes and learn from them. This doesn't mean we've failed; it means we get to begin again. And this applies to every aspect of our lives—physical, intellectual, emotional, and spiritual.

I think of each life as a gift like a candle. The length of the candle at any given time doesn't represent one's age, but how much of our designated time that we have left. Our job is to illuminate the path for ourselves and for others. We must not worry about how much time we have, but just concentrate on doing the candle's job to the best of our ability. When we're done with any part of our life, whether that is a job, a relationship, or some goal, we shouldn't blow out the wick and let the wax grow cold. We need to use every bit of the gift we are—and use it well. We need to burn up and not out before our time is up. If we always see life as a series of endings, we limit life's possibilities. Someone who turns 65 and gets the retirement party, for example, might think, *I'm not useful anymore.* Another person diagnosed with cancer or heart disease might react with *My life is over.* When we see life through an ending lens and someone we love dies, we see the whole relationship ending. But this isn't the case. Love goes on. We don't stop loving them just because they're dead, and we don't stop feeling their love for us. When we see life as a series of beginnings, our lives change and grow and move from one stage to another. It's as if the word becomes a sentence, the paragraph a page, the chapter a book, and so on. Life just doesn't stop.

We also tend to think of ourselves as being created—not as creating ourselves—especially as we grow older and the end of our lives seems to loom ever closer. We think, *I am a doctor, I am a husband, I am a father and grandfather,* and we forget that there are many more "I ams" ahead, many roles to fill, things to learn, and talents to discover. One example of this begins in my younger years. In the four years of college prior to medical school, I had top grades in everything except creative writing. I never got higher than a C on my writing assignments. The only C I received in college was the grade for that class! I know now that this was the result of my intellectual approach to writing. I wrote the assignments from my head, not my heart. I thought about the topic too much and didn't tap into my feelings and intuition or just let the words flow out of me. Because of my low grade, I came to believe that I was not a writer. Years later, a patient of mine who happened to be a psychic-mystic told me that I would write several books. I thought she was nuts at the time, but she was right.

One day I realized that in order to educate and inspire people to make real changes in the world, I had to reach a much greater audience. The only way I could see to do that was to write a book, and so began my life as an author. That I even became a writer proves there is hope for everybody. When we change from believing what we're told to believing our intuitions and hearts instead, we create the potential for our lives to change. Today "I am" the author of several bestsellers, all of them written after getting that C grade.

After my first book, *Love, Medicine & Miracles,* became a #1 *New York Times* bestseller, I wrote to Colgate University asking them to raise my C grade to a B so I could be a summa cum laude graduate. My childlike sense of humor instigates me to do these things. In their return letter, there was no humor, only the statement that they couldn't raise my grades after graduation. I felt sorry for them; imagine taking life and my letter so seriously.

When you create your Bible II, don't think of it as just one book or journal. Think of it as a series of notebooks you can keep adding to. A ring binder allows you to place your collection of quotes, stories, and wisdom into sections or categories. Make sure to leave a big space for humor, and include letters like the one I got from the university.

It is my hope that we will all dedicate ourselves to serving God's purpose and truly sense that God is aware of us and of everything we do. I hope we will enter each day with the curiosity and wonder of a scientist who begins his experiments with an open mind and a sense of humor. In living this way, we play a much greater part in creation as it is happening—far more than the individual with narrow interests. We get to see that there really are no ends, only beginnings. It is why graduations are called commencements, terminations are transformations, and the Bible ends with a Revelation and not a conclusion.

In this section we will look at life's graduations and commencements from the aspects of living, dying, grieving, and healing. Are you prepared to leave behind what you should already know? Then open your senses, turn the page, and *let's begin!*

Heal Your Life and Be Happy

Our childhood is stored up in our body and although we can repress it and treat it with medications, someday the body will present its bill. For it is as incorruptible as a child who, while still whole in spirit, will not stop tormenting us until we stop evading the truth.

– **Alice Miller** (1923–2010),
Swiss psychologist and author of *The Body Never Lies*

Alice Miller's lifelong work dealing with the long-ranging consequences of childhood trauma completely overturned the thinking and therapeutic approach of professionals in psychology, medicine, and human development after World War II. When children experience trauma or abuse, one of their greatest coping mechanisms is to encase the emotions—and often the memory of such events—by storing them in the body or in the consciousness of an alternate personality. This gives the vulnerable child a chance to deal with the feelings later, when they feel safe from harm, are old enough to make sense of what happened, and have some power over their lives. But if they keep these things buried and never face the truth of their past experiences and feelings by working through them with the help of therapeutic counseling, they will suffer eruptions of mental, physical, and social health problems for the rest of their lives. And the consequences of unresolved trauma can and do affect later generations.

Health is the natural state, the default program of our bodies. We were designed to maintain and recover to this state. When people become ill, whether physically or mentally, it can be a sign that they have lost their health because something in their lives that is, or was, harmful to them has not been dealt with. Doctors can treat symptoms and remove or cure certain diseases, but individuals who don't heal problematic circumstances in their lives—whether those circumstances were in the past or are happening in the present—remain susceptible to losing their health again.

Many people avoid psychological therapy for fear of what will happen when the strong emotions they've buried rise to the surface. But healthy, appropriate anger is essential to the healing process. The Bible speaks of righteous indignation. Sometimes anger is required for you to survive when you are not treated with respect. The word *patient* implies being a submissive sufferer, and that is not survival behavior. Strong emotions that have been stored for a long time need to be exposed and expressed with the help of counseling or therapy. They can literally kill you. So always give yourself permission to speak up when you are not treated properly and seek help without shame or fear.

Suicidal thinking is the last symptom, the result of being unable to see a way out of anguish. I used to ask my students to do the following exercise, and I suggest you do it too: write a suicide note, and then a love note, as if you were writing to yourself. To do this, sit down and think, *What reasons are there for me to commit suicide? Why would I want to end my life?* When that is done, write yourself the love note.

When I ask students to do this exercise, they average eight pages on why they ought to be dead and only three paragraphs on why they are lovable. When the students realize they are not alone in these feelings, the class suicide rate goes down because they stop hiding the truth, share their wounds, and help each other to heal. If your suicide note is several pages and your love note is only a few paragraphs, it is time to stop and look at your life.

Eliminate the parts of your life that are destroying you; don't eliminate yourself. And please, give your children self-worth and -esteem. Help them to eliminate the part of their lives they don't like so they won't wish to end their lives. I found that patients who didn't die when they were "supposed to" always had a story to tell me about major changes they made in their lives. They didn't deny their mortality; they just started living. There were times, a year or so after a terminal patient was sent home to die, I'd call to ask the family why I wasn't invited to the funeral only for the person I thought was dead to answer the phone and tell me they had quit their career, moved to their dream place, started a wildlife habitat, or changed their life to something they loved. Now they were so happy they had forgotten to die.

Remember the words of Jesus: "He who loses his life will save it." When you are living not *your* life but the one imposed on you, you lose yourself. Eliminate the false you and save your life, like the doctor who learns he has cancer, gives up his medical practice, and plays the flute in an orchestra—something he has always wanted to do. The doctor dies, but the musician survives.

Spiritual or hands-on healing can be quite powerful in shifting energy, as are many alternative treatments like acupuncture and homeopathy. I encourage people to try alternatives as well as conventional medicine, but let the doctors and practitioners know so they can work together as a team. Prayer is also a form of therapy when it is a request for strength, resourcefulness, direction, and awareness. It is powerful when it thanks God for what has been given you. Prayer can also be getting tough with God, saying clearly what you want now and then placing your life in God's hands. One of my patients went home to die due to the extent of her disease—a large abdominal tumor you could feel. When she returned to the office two months later with no sign of cancer, she said, "I left my troubles to God."

Incredible healing power and potential happen when faith and hope are working together. Hope literally enhances the life force. I have been criticized for giving false hope to patients. False hope is an oxymoron; it just can't exist. It is not about lying to patients, it's about increasing possibilities and probabilities. People win the lottery despite the poor odds. Some doctors called my Exceptional Cancer Patients (ECaP) group members "crazy patients" because people with every type of disease in this group were responding better to treatments, felt happier, and were dying with more acceptance. One woman with terminal cancer wanted to come up from North Carolina to join our group, and her oncologist said to me, "I agree with her doctor that she has little time left to live, but I know you and your crazy patients, so I will give her hope." Two months later she was in complete remission from her leukemia. Her comment: "I knew I would get well when Dr.

Siegel sat on my bed and hugged me." The oncologist responded, "Isn't chemotherapy wonderful?" Treatment is not about holding on to the limited belief of why we cannot be healed. When we believe in our treatment, and when our doctors or therapists believe in our treatment, positive outcomes are significantly higher.

So have faith in your body, talk to God, and live with hope. If you have none, seek help. Identify and eliminate the cause of your dis-ease. As Miller says, don't medicate yourself to repress the past. Write yourself a love letter, and give yourself permission to do *whatever* it takes to heal your life and live.

Don't See Death as a Failure

The day will come when . . . my life has stopped.

When that happens . . . let my body be taken . . .
to help others lead fuller lives.

Give my sight to the man who has never seen
a sunrise, a baby's face or love in the eyes
of a woman.

Give my heart to a person whose own heart has
caused nothing but endless days of pain.

Give my blood to the teenager who was pulled
from the wreckage of his car, so that he might live
to see his grandchildren play.

Give my kidneys to the one who depends on a
machine to exist from week to week.

Take my bones, every muscle, every fiber and
nerve in my body and find a way to make a
crippled child walk.

Explore every corner of my brain. Take my cells,
if necessary, and let them grow so that someday
a speechless boy will shout at the crack of a bat
and a deaf girl will hear the sound of rain against
her windows.

Burn what is left of me and scatter the ashes to the
winds to help the flowers grow.

> If you must bury something, let it be my faults, my weaknesses and all prejudice against my fellow man.
>
> Give my sins to the devil. Give my soul to God. If, by chance, you wish to remember me, do it with a kind deed or word to someone who needs you. If you do all I have asked, I will live forever.
>
> – **Robert Noel Test** (1926–1994), American pioneer in promoting organ and tissue donation

The excerpt above was taken from the essay "To Remember Me," written by Robert Test during his lunch break. He once said he wrote it just for the fun of it. This proves my point that when you do what you love doing, your life becomes meaningful. The essay has inspired innumerable people to sign on as organ donors and families to donate the bodies of their loved ones. The grieving family's loving act of releasing their beloved's body—in order that others may live—has given them great comfort, even when they first balked at the idea of doing such a thing. The death is no longer meaningless to them, for something good came out of their tragedy, and a part of their beloved still lives.

For most of us, the darkest spot we face in life is our death. The fear of the unknown leads us to lose our innocence. I say for most because, for those who have lived with it, thought about it, and faced it, death may even be the brightest spot of all. I was talking with some terminal patients about life and its difficulties when one of them said, "Dying isn't the worst outcome," and another, nodding in agreement, replied, "I can survive dying." Laughter filled the room. But the truth is we can. Living is a lot harder than dying.

Impending death may not only enlighten us but at some point become our therapy. Mortality is a greater teacher and enlightener than anything else. There is a time to leave our bodies, just as there is a time to enter them. And death is a form of healing when we leave a body that we can no longer use to love with. Our death is a commencement, not a termination. Richard Bach, author of *Jonathan Livingston Seagull* and several inspiring metaphysical novels, had another way of putting it: "What the caterpillar calls the end of the world, the master calls a butterfly."

We all know how impending death can affect the family and friends of the dying, but we forget that it challenges the medical team as well. A medical student who spent a month working with me interviewed 25 physicians concerning their attitudes about death. At the conclusion of the paper reporting his findings, he wrote: "It is important to come to an acceptance of death not only as an absolute reality, but as part of the natural order of things. When the physician achieves this acceptance, he or she no longer needs to avoid the people who have problems that he cannot solve. [He or she] is then able to remain in a partnership with the patient and to share the common bond of mortality and love that they have between them until the very end."

Remember, beating a disease is not about being cured; it's about not letting the disease ruin your life. I hear from people with all kinds of difficulties talking about the effort of winning, losing, beating it, or battling it. But know this: You are not a loser if you die. Death is not a failure. It is the effort put into living and dying that is important. As a man who died of ALS said, "What's wrong with being number two?" He spoke those words to the audience at a college game while the students were all screaming "We're number one." We need to focus on healing, not fighting, because the fight empowers our enemy.

When he was in his late 70s, my father-in-law, Ado, got new bifocals. Because he couldn't see distance clearly through the bottom of the lenses, he missed a step and fell off his back porch. Subsequently he became a quadriplegic. On one of our visits, I told him I was going to give a lecture to seniors. Did he have any words of wisdom to share? He replied, "Tell them to fall on something soft." A few days later he said, "That doesn't always work because when they stood me up in therapy, I fell on my wife and broke her leg, so tell them to just fall up." Ado was such a wonderful man I wanted him to live to be 100 and be interviewed on the news, which wasn't fair of me, for his body had become like a prison. He could have lived in misery and dragged everybody around him down, but he kept looking on the bright side and gave everybody something to laugh about. A cheerful attitude is a wonderful gift to share when your body no longer works. One day, when he was 97, Ado refused his pills and dinner and died peacefully in his sleep that night. He left us with so many happy memories, and we had his headstone engraved with the words "He just fell up."

So remember, life isn't a battle; it's a series of choices. Life is not about fighting death; it is about the relationships, humor, joy, and vitality. The best way to ensure that your death is not a failure is to participate fully in life now. Believe me—you aren't dead as long as you are alive. If you haven't done so yet, sign on as an organ donor. Take care of your body so it will last for two lifetimes. Let your death be a blessing for others and your reward for a life well lived.

Grieve, Laugh, Love, and Live

I didn't want to know grief.
But the pain kept me connected.
It meant that I loved you,
It meant that I would always be a little broken,
It meant that our love filled all of the empty spaces.
It meant that you would be with me . . . forever.

– **Dr. Jacqueline Simon Gunn**,
Clinical Psychologist and Author

Grieving is important, healthy, and necessary, but sometimes we hold on to grief for too long. As the excerpt from Dr. Gunn's poem "Empty Spaces" shows, many of us see our grief as being the last thing we have that connects us with our loved ones. Letting go of the grief in this circumstance feels like we're letting go of them—an impossible thing to face. Yet, in order to go on living in any meaningful way, we must eventually let go of the grief, for holding on to it blocks the joy of having had our loved ones' presence in our lives.

We may need to seek help through grief counseling, support groups, and so on. "Who would I be without this grief?" is a good question to meditate on after writing about the pain or before doing some other form of creative work.

Being present with loved ones when they die can help us to begin the process of grieving, especially if those last moments are filled with laughter and the companionship of close friends and family. Several years ago my father said to my mother, "Rose, I need to get out of here." Her interpretation of his words was that he didn't like the side rails on the hospital bed. I said, "Mom, his statement has more to do with his body than the side rails and getting out of bed." She spoke to him then, saying it was okay to leave his body. We asked him when he wanted to die, and he picked the next Sunday, so we organized his party by notifying everyone Grampa would be dying Sunday and asking who was coming to the party.

By the following Sunday, Dad had fallen into a coma. Our son Jonathan, who was with him, called early in the morning to say it looked like he was dying and we had best come now. I didn't jump in the car and race to get there. I knew Dad would wait, so I went out for my hour alone, and as I was running, the voice said, "How did your parents meet?" I answered, "I don't know." The voice instructed, "Then ask your mother when you get to the hospital."

My parents had been married over 60 years, and you might think in all those years I would have heard them talking about their early life together. But I hadn't. Because of the voice, I knew it was important to ask. When Bobbie and I walked into Dad's hospital room, and before I could say anything compassionate to Mom, I blurted out, "How did you two meet?"

My mother's sad expression changed, and as she smiled, a younger version of herself looked out through sparkling eyes. She then began to tell us a story about being on summer vacation with her family. She had been sitting on the beach at Far Rockaway, New York City, with several teenage girls, whom she had just met. "I later learned they had a very bad reputation," Mom said. "Coming down the beach were a bunch of young men, including your father, who knew the other girls. They tossed coins to see who would get the other girls. Your father lost and got me."

We all began to laugh and continued laughing as she rolled out the stories. On their next date, Dad took her for a row in Central Park. Mom put her foot in the boat, and as my father turned to pay the man, he let go of my mother's hand. At that moment the boat left the dock, and Mom fell into the water. Their early dates were just one humorous disaster after another. As Mom related these memories, Dad began to smile. Even though he was in a coma, he heard every word. I know from my experience as a doctor and surgeon that we continue to hear even when we are in a coma, asleep, or under anesthesia. Dad looked so healthy and alive I thought he was going to change his mind about dying while my mother continued to tell their stories.

My father could not know consciously who the last person to arrive was going to be. Some of his grandchildren living in Florida and California were unable to get there that day. As we waited for the rest of the family to arrive, we shared the laughter and love, and when the last grandchild who could come entered his room, Dad took a breath and died. I can accept that Dad's consciousness knew who to wait for and who wasn't coming. Bobbie, who was seated near the foot of Dad's bed, saw a ripple rise up from his body and leave at that moment. It was 3 p.m., and he was surrounded by the people who loved him.

I later found an interview of mine in which I had said it would be lovely if we could die at three in the afternoon surrounded by our loved ones—not alone in the middle of the night. My father never read or heard that interview, but his spirit did. The ending of his physical life was a beautiful experience, and my father left with no guilt. Not a single child went out of the hospital room with a fear of death.

After my mother died, I found over two dozen pennies in the oddest places. They appeared everywhere with no explanation. At times I would walk to the mailbox and see none but find several on the way back up the drive. My mother's great-grandchildren called these "pennies from heaven." This is now a common and expected event in our family after someone's death.

When we know our beloved is going to die soon, we begin the grief process even though their actual death may be weeks or months away. In a sense, their death happens for us every morning as we wake and every night as we go to bed, wondering if they'll be gone when we next see them. This is difficult if we're also trying to be strong for others and not darken the last days we have with our beloved. It helps during this period to turn to God. Someone I knew through a cancer group said he knew there was a God, he just didn't think he needed Him. Many of us live that way until difficulties arise. It's only then that we realize the power of prayer and the role of the spiritual and the Creator in our lives. Remember, you are God's child, so let your Father help out when you need Him. Also, speak with someone supportive and write about your feelings of being left behind.

When I began to see Bobbie's life diminishing, I wrote the following poem:

THE CLOCK OF LIFE

I rested my head on the chest of my wife,
And heard her heart ticking away our life.
How many beats in a lifetime?
I wish I could slow the pace.
I could listen to her heart forever.
How precious the sound—a strong steady beat,
Like our life together:
Only an occasional skip,
And then our regular rhythm returns.

Bobbie, my sweetheart and wife of 63 years, died on the 19th of January 2018. When I entered her room in the morning, I saw a spirit cloud over her body. In the hours and days after, I was hoping to see some sign of her presence, some confirmation that she was still with us. One morning as I was walking our dog, Rags, in the woods, I told Bobbie I needed some help and asked her for a penny. The very next day I found a penny on the ground in the exact same spot where I had stopped the day before.

From then on "pennies from heaven" showed up everywhere: in the woods while walking the dog; at the Stop & Shop checkout counter and parking lot; inside our house and out; and even one in a birdbath beside our house. Another penny appeared on the podium where I gave a lecture. I found it after I had finished my talk and was gathering up my papers. It had not been there earlier when I had placed my notes down and started to speak.

Celestial treasures have continued to appear ever since. No less than five times, I have found 11 cents—a dime and a penny together—in bizarre locations. Eleven is significant because Bobbie and I were married on the 11th of July. When our first anniversary without her came around, this was the message on my calendar for July 11th: "A part of you has grown in me, and so you see, it's you and me, together forever and never apart, maybe in distance, but never in heart." Also on the 11th, my watch stopped running for no apparent reason and displayed that date into the following day, when it started working again. Bobbie's birthdate was 9/9, the 9th of September. In September I started having an irregular heartbeat, called fibrillation, and in October I was hospitalized because of the arrhythmia. I knew it was my heart's response to the loss of my loved one. I was taken to the emergency room at

Yale New Haven Hospital and heard them say, "Put him in Room 9." And the next morning I was moved to hospital room number 819. The 8 is a new beginning and infinity symbol according to Jung. When I see it, I know I will be okay. All my patient identification numbers added up to nine.

Whenever I go back for checkups, I am assigned a new patient number, and each time the numbers add up to nine or our anniversary date. When I see these signs, I know Bobbie is still there looking out for me, helping to heal my broken heart. To help me get through the days, she also posts healing messages in her own mystical way where I live and work. The other day there was a butterfly in the house, and it woke me up banging on a window. So I picked it up gently—it showed no fear—and I released it outside. Again I can't explain how it got into the house and why it was quiet all night. Leave it to Bobbie.

I speak from experience and love when I say the pain of grief will pull you in all directions, but don't become directionless. Don't let your tears put out their celestial candles. Move toward transcendence. Find the lessons in the wealth of grief. Don't refuse to suffer and only distract yourself to feel better. Instead, participate in the journey. Accept your sorrow as a tree accepts water. Take it in, grow with it, and grow from it. Remember Dr. Gunn's words, that you'll "always be a little broken" but that your "love will fill the empty spaces." Be grateful for your beloved who lived and keep living for the love of them.

Hold On

So the darkness shall be the light, and the stillness the dancing.

– **T. S. Eliot** (1888–1965),
English poet, essayist, playwright, and publisher

In the quiet moments, when I'm not exercising the dogs, visiting family, giving lectures, or working on my books and website, the void left by Bobbie's physical absence is greater than I could ever have imagined. Eliot's words successfully portray the limbo state, the waiting, I sometimes feel myself slipping into these days. I always wanted to live to be 120, but now, in my 80s, I often wonder when I'll be reunited with Bobbie. It feels better when I'm busy and best of all when I'm helping others. Yet I must admit there is a dancing in the stillness and a light in the darkness, for that is where I feel her presence most closely.

I talk to her throughout the day, and I look through our old letters and notes. Those memories fill me with a sense of warmth and laughter that are truly comforting, and I keep having incredible mystical experiences. One night I heard Bobbie making sounds next to me in bed, so I sat up and asked her, "Do you need any help?" Then I chuckled and said to myself, "Hey, dumbbell, she's dead." Years ago, using Bobbie's lipstick, I drew a heart with an arrow on our bathroom window, with the words "I Love You" inside the heart. It is still there, and every morning the sunlight casts its shadow onto the bathroom floor. I know she is still with me.

I am so grateful for all the opportunities life gave to us and for the sense of guidance we often felt when we most needed it. Bobbie always used to say, "Believe in what you experience." In these last paragraphs, I will share with you a couple of examples of those times when we felt we were led by a force greater than us. And last of all, I'll share a memory that makes me laugh and gives me the sense of Bobbie still here, looking over my shoulder, waiting to plant a big kiss on my cheek.

Many years ago, Bobbie and I were going to give a talk, and we followed the directions that someone had given us to reach the place. We became totally lost and came to the end of the road, with just a stone wall facing us. We didn't know where to turn. At that moment a car pulled up in front of us with license plates that read, "IM LOST." We knew that car was sent for us, so we spoke to the drivers and they kindly led us to our destination.

Another time we were in California and had rented a car, but we didn't know how to get to the place we were headed. I stopped a man on the street and asked him how to get to Berkeley Street. He replied he had no idea, but he told me where there was a police station where I might get help. When we drove to the police station, guess what? It was on Berkeley Street. These incidents were no coincidence. They happened so many times we always knew something or someone would come along and guide us.

When I worked at the hospital, Bobbie made lunch for me every day. She would fill a red lunch box—one with the word *love* printed in white all over the entire box—and she would put a love note in with the sandwich and fruit. On a very stressful and difficult day for me, a day filled with emergencies, I didn't find time to eat until the late afternoon. When I opened my lunch box, there was the usual note from her, but this time all it said was "HOLD ON."

I thought how fortunate I was to have an intuitive wife who knew I would be having a tough day and would send me just the right message. She always added the symbolic hugs and kisses, XOXOXOXO, but this note contained no other words or direction. When I got home, I went directly to her and started thanking her for being so intuitive. I told her how her note had really helped me get through the day.

Bobbie asked, "What are you talking about?"

"Your message to 'HOLD ON,'" I replied. "Your words inspired me. I did hold on, and I made it through a very difficult day."

Bobbie then said, "It was a big sandwich with a lot of vegetables. I just wanted you to hold on with both hands so you wouldn't have a mess on your lap."

From then on, her messages read, "This is a two-hand sandwich."

So I ask you to remember Bobbie's note and, whenever life gets difficult, use two hands and just HOLD ON. If you have an accident with a ladder or a horse, notice what you shout as you're falling, and remember, that's your angel's name. I also hope you will, if you haven't already, start collecting meaningful phrases and poems and record your stories. Let this book be an inspiration for you to find—in your stillness—the dancing.

I will leave you now with a few of Bobbie's words. You might want to borrow them one day and make someone you love feel special. Several years ago, I framed one of her old lunch box notes and hung it on the bathroom wall, where it still hangs. It reads:

"You must be putting something in the water to make me want to live with you."

When I was going through my desk to gather quotes for this book, another lunch box note fell out and landed on my lap. I picked it up and read Bobbie's neat handwriting:

"I love you, you crazy person."

ONE LAST QUOTE

I do dimly perceive that, whilst everything around me is ever changing, ever dying, there is—underlying all that change—a living power that is changeless, that holds all together, that creates, dissolves, and re-creates. That informing power of spirit is God. And since nothing else that I see merely through the senses can—or will—persist, He alone is. And is this power benevolent or malevolent? I see it as purely benevolent, for I can see that in the midst of death, life persists; in the midst of untruth, truth persists; in the midst of darkness, light persists. Hence I gather that God is Life, Truth, Light. He is Love. He is the supreme Good.

– **Mahatma Gandhi** (1869-1948),
Indian lawyer, activist, and leader of the Indian independence movement

Gandhi's words speak so clearly of the message I have tried to share with you—the message that connecting us all, holding *everything in existence* together is a loving, benevolent consciousness that never ends; it just keeps creating anew. Now, in the quiet moments when I listen for God's voice, I am reassured and comforted by the vision he shares—that our time as spiritually blind and deaf human beings is nearing its end. The great classroom of human experience as we know it is approaching commencement. Soon we will all be raised from the darkness of ignorance and forgetfulness. The veil will be lifted, and we will see ourselves as we truly are. Every one of us will return home to be embraced by life, truth, light, and love. So have faith, and HOLD ON.

Bernie Siegel
28th April 2019

ENDNOTES

Introduction

xi "Make your own Bible. Select and collect all those words and sentences . . ." Ralph Waldo Emerson, quoted in Robert D. Richardson Jr., "Emerson as Editor," in *Emersonian Circles: Essays in Honor of Joel Myerson*, ed. Wesley T. Mott and Robert E. Burkholder (New York: University of Rochester Press, 1997), 110.

1. Begin Your Quest for Truth

1 "Where is God in all of this? You ask yourself, head in your hands . . ." Charlie Siegel, "The Answer Lies Within" (unpublished poem).

5 "Remember that you are an actor in a play, and the Playwright chooses the manner of it . . ." Epictetus, *The Manual* 17, in *The Discourses and Manual*, trans. P. E. Matheson (New York: Heritage Press, 1968), 279.

8 "There is no such thing as learning to be whole without being tested . . ." Clarissa Pinkola Estés, *Untie the Strong Woman: Blessed Mother's Immaculate Love for the Wild Soul* (Boulder: Sounds True, 2001), 333.

11 "The violets of patience and sweetness . . ."Helen Keller, *My Religion* (San Diego: The Book Tree, 2007), 186.

14 "We are surrounded by an Infinite Possibility. It is Goodness, Life, Law and Reason . . ." Ernest S. Holmes, *The Essential Ernest Holmes: Collected Writings*, ed. Jesse Jennings (New York: Penguin Putnam, 2002), 63.

2. Live Authentically

21 "We are more than a body and a brain: we are also a soul and spirit. . . ." Robert Moss, *Dreaming the Soul Back Home* (Novato, CA: New World Library, 2012), 1.

25 "[To attempt] to be 'normal' is a splendid ideal for the unsuccessful, for all those . . ." Carl Gustav Jung, *Modern Man in Search of a Soul*, trans. W. S. Dell and Cary F. Baynes (London: Routledge Classics, 2001), 48.

28 "Practice, practice, practice . . ." Jane Wagner, *Search for Signs of Intelligent Life in the Universe* (1979).

31 "Words saturated with sincerity, conviction, faith, and intuition . . ." Paramahansa Yogananda, *Self-realization* 58 (1986): 54.

37 "As the poets and painters of centuries have tried to tell us, art is not about the expression of talent . . ." Thomas Moore, *Care of the Soul* (London: Judy Pratkus, 1992).

3. Be an Agent of Change

45 "In archery we have something like the way of the superior man. When the archer . . ." Confucius, *The Doctrine of the Mean*, trans. James Legge (Shanghai: Commercial Press, 1930), chap. 14:5, https://fliphtml5.com/bbhu/tgie.

51 "Nothing in the world is as soft and yielding as water, yet for dissolving the hard . . ." Lao-tzu, Tao Te Ching, trans. Stephen Mitchell (New York: Harper Collins, 1988) chap. 78. Retrieved from: https://cpb-us-w2.wpmucdn.com/u.osu.edu/dist/5/25851/files/2016/02/taoteching-Stephen-Mitchell-translation-v9deoq.pdf.

58 "When you stand in front of me and look at me, what do you know of the griefs . . ." Franz Kafka to Oskar Pollak, November 8, 1903, in *Briefe 1902–1924*, ed. Max Brod (1958), 27.

63 "Seek goodness everywhere, and when it is found, bring it out of its hiding-place . . ." William Saroyan, introduction to *The Time of Your Life* (San Diego: Harcourt Brace, 1939).

4. Seek the Creator Everywhere

71 "Apprehend God in all things, / For God is in all things. / Every single creature . . ." Meister Eckhart, commentary on Eccles., in Sermon 9, "Predigten Quint 9," *Deutsche Werke*, vol. 1 (Stuttgart: Kolhammer, 1958), 156, quoted in Lisa Kemmerer, *Animals and World Religions* (New York: Oxford University Press, 2012), 201n.

74 "Just ask the animals, and they will teach you . . ." Job 12:7–8 (New Living Translation).

80 "The eyes of the animal contain the truth of life, an equal sum of pain and pleasure . . ." Carl Gustav Jung, *Letters*, vol. 2 (Princeton University Press, 1973), 486.

86 "And your ears shall hear a voice behind you, saying, This is the way; walk in it." Isaiah 30:21.

5. Just Love

93 "In the time of your life, live—so that in that wondrous time you shall not add . . ." William Saroyan, introduction to *The Time of Your Life* (San Diego: Harcourt Brace, 1939).

96 "Love is the medicine for our sick old world. If people can learn to give and receive . . ." Karl Menninger, *A Psychiatrist's World: The Selected Papers of Karl Menninger, M.D.* (New York: Viking Press, 1959), 49.

102 "If I can stop one heart from breaking, / I shall not live in vain; / If I can ease one life . . ." Emily Dickinson, "If I Can Stop One Heart from Breaking," in *The Complete Poems of Emily Dickinson* (Pantianos Classics, 1924), 10.

108 "A friend of mine, an industrialist in a large plant in Ohio, told me . . ." Norman Vincent Peale, *The Power of Positive Thinking* (London: Vermillion, 2012), 45.

115 "We prayed so that all bitterness could be taken from us and we could start . . ." Laurens van der Post, *A Far Off Place* (London: Hogarth Press, 1974), 43.

6. Explore the Mysteries

121 "BUT I WOULD LIKE TO KNOW WHAT I MYSELF CAN KNOW . . ." Ernest S. Holmes and Fenwicke L. Holmes, "Reverie of the Farer," in *The Voice Celestial: An Epic Poem* (New York: Dodd, Mead, 1960).

127 "There is something peculiar, one might even say mysterious, about numbers . . ." Carl Gustav Jung, trans. R. F.C. Hull, *Synchronicity: An Acausal Connecting Principle* (London: Routledge, 1955), 57.

131 "A coin / the body has minted, with an invisible motto . . ." John Updike, "Ode to Healing," in *Merrimack: A Poetry Anthology*, ed. Kathleen Aponick (Lowell, MA: Loom Press, 1992), 115.

133 "Man was so created by the Lord as to be able while living in the body to speak . . ." Emanuel Swedenborg, trans. John Clowes, *Arcana Coelestia: Volume 1 – The Arcane Edition* (Loschburg, Germany: Jazzybee Verlag, 2013), 70.

138 "Meaningful coincidences are thinkable as pure chance. But the more they multiply . . ." Carl Gustav Jung, *The Collected Works of C. G. Jung*, vol. 8, *The Structure & Dynamics of the Psyche* (Princeton University Press, 1981), 518.

144 "To know that we maintain an identity independent of the physical body is proof . . ." Ernest S. Holmes, *The Science of Mind* (New York: Dodd, Mead, 1938), 377.

7. Share Your Stories

151 "The new discoveries of science 'rejoin us to the ancients' by enabling us to recognize . . ." Bill Moyers, introduction to *The Power of Myth*, by Joseph Campbell with Bill Moyers (New York: Anchor Books, 1988), xix.

156 "Try to remember that a good man can never die. You will see him many times . . ." William Saroyan, *The Human Comedy* (New York: Harcourt Brace, 1943), 275.

158 "The death rate for infants under a year old . . ." Ashley Montagu, *Touching: The Human Significance of the Skin* (New York: Harper Collins, 1986).

163 "But each absorbed in each, and each in one, / Through love are merged . . ." Ernest S. Holmes and Fenwicke L. Holmes, from "The Scribe" in *The Voice Celestial: An Epic Poem* (New York: Dodd, Mead, 1960).

168 "Sufficient unto the day is one baby . . ." Mark Twain, "Speech on the Babies," The Literature Network, accessed July 7, 2019, http://www.online-literature.com/twain/3274/. Taken from Mark Twain's speech prior to raising his glass in toast at a banquet in Chicago, where the Tennessee Regiment of the army honored their First Commander, General Ulysses S. Grant, in November 1879. The 15th regular toast was "The Babies—as they comfort us in our sorrows, let us not forget them in our festivities."

8. Understand That Endings Are Always Beginnings

177 "When you reach the end of what you should know . . ." Kahlil Gibran, *Sand and Foam and Other Poems* (Oxford: Benediction, 2010), 27.

182 "Our childhood is stored up in our body and although we can repress . . ." Alice Miller, *Breaking Down the Wall of Silence: The Liberating Experience of Facing Painful Truth* (New York: Penguin, 1996), 153.

189 "The day will come when . . . my life has stopped. / When that happens . . ." Robert Noel Test, "To Remember Me," quoted in Abigail Van Buren, "A Great Way to Be Remembered," *Chicago Tribune*, April 17, 1995, https://www.chicagotribune.com/news/ct-xpm-1995-04-17-9504170019-story.html. Test donated his essay to promote tissue and organ donation.

193 "I didn't want to know grief. / But the pain kept me connected . . ." Jacqueline Simon Gunn, "Empty Spaces," Jacqueline Simon Gunn's blog, April 2, 2017, http://www.jsgunn.com/blog/2017/4/2/empty-spaces-1.

202 "So the darkness shall be the light, and the stillness the dancing." T. S. Eliot, "East Coker," from *Four Quartets*, in *The Complete Poems and Plays: 1909–1950* (Orlando: Harcourt Brace, 1952), 126–27.

One Last Quote

207 "I do dimly perceive that, whilst everything around me is ever changing . . ." Mahatma Gandhi at Kingsley Hall, London, 1931," YouTube video, 6:05, October 12, 2016, https://www.youtube.com/watch?v=oE2Z4wLxw80. Mahatma Gandhi's address to a large gathering at Kingsley Hall, London, was given on October 17, 1931. He later called this speech "My Spiritual Message."

ACKNOWLEDGMENTS

I primarily want to acknowledge my creators for their empowering wisdom and love: my wife, Bobbie; my parents, Si and Rose; and our children, Jon, Jeff, Steve, Carolyn, and Keith.

I also wish to thank and acknowledge the work of my co-author, Cynthia Hurn; my editor, Allison Janice; and my agent, Andrea Hurst. And I certainly want to thank God.

Bernie Siegel, M.D.

ABOUT THE AUTHORS

Bernie S. Siegel, M.D.

Retired surgeon Bernie S. Siegel is a well-known proponent of integrative and holistic approaches to healing not just the body, but also the mind and soul. Bernie, as his friends and patients call him, attended Colgate University and studied medicine at Cornell University Medical College. His surgical training took place at Yale New Haven Hospital, West Haven Veterans Hospital, and the Children's Hospital of Pittsburgh. In 1978 Bernie pioneered a new approach to group and individual cancer therapy called Exceptional Cancer Patients (ECaP), which utilized patients' drawings, dreams, and feelings, and he broke new ground in facilitating important lifestyle changes and engaging the patient in the healing process.

Bernie retired from his general and pediatric surgical practice in 1989. Always a strong advocate for his patients, he has since dedicated himself to humanizing the medical establishment's approach to patients and empowering patients to play a vital role in the process of self-induced healing to achieve their greatest potential. He continues to run support groups and is an active speaker, traveling around the world to address patient and caregiver groups. As the author of several books—including *Love, Medicine & Miracles*; *How to Live Between Office Visits*; *365 Prescriptions for the Soul*; *The Art of Healing*; and *Love, Animals & Miracles*—Bernie has been at the forefront of spiritual and medical ethics issues of our day. He has been named one of the top 20 Most Spiritually Influential Living People by Watkins' *Mind Body Spirit* magazine (London). Bernie, now a widower, has five children and eight grandchildren. He lives in a suburb of New Haven, Connecticut, with his four cats, one dog, and Bobbie's spirit and soul.

Visit his website at www.berniesiegelmd.com.

Cynthia J. Hurn

Freelance writer and editor Cynthia J. Hurn is co-author of the nonfiction books *No Buddy Left Behind: Bringing U.S. Troops' Dogs and Cats Safely Home from the Combat Zone*; *The Art of Healing*; *Not My Secret to Keep: A Memoir of Healing from Childhood Sexual Abuse*; and *Love, Animals & Miracles*, and author of the metaphysical historical novel *The Shimmering*. Her studies in psychology, counseling, and creative writing, plus volunteer work with animals and rescued wild birds, bring a unique mixture of science, heart, and soul to her writing. Her books have won multiple awards. In 2014, Cynthia founded Café Write, a writer's group in Somerset, England. She lives with her golden retriever, Worthy, and Romanian rescue dog, Rosie, at her home in Port Townsend, Washington.

To contact, e-mail cjhurn@gmail.com and include the title of this book in the subject line.

Hay House Titles of Related Interest

YOU CAN HEAL YOUR LIFE, the movie,
starring Louise Hay & Friends
(available as a 1-DVD program, an expanded 2-DVD set,
and an online streaming video)
Learn more at www.hayhouse.com/louise-movie

THE SHIFT, the movie,
starring Dr. Wayne W. Dyer
(available as a 1-DVD program, an expanded 2-DVD set,
and an online streaming video)
Learn more at www.hayhouse.com/the-shift-movie

We hope you enjoyed this Hay House book. If you'd like to receive our online catalog featuring additional information on Hay House books and products, or if you'd like to find out more about the Hay Foundation, please contact:

Hay House, Inc., P.O. Box 5100, Carlsbad, CA 92018-5100
(760) 431-7695 or (800) 654-5126
(760) 431-6948 (fax) or (800) 650-5115 (fax)
www.hayhouse.com® • www.hayfoundation.org

Published in Australia by: Hay House Australia Pty. Ltd., 18/36 Ralph St., Alexandria NSW 2015
Phone: 612-9669-4299 • *Fax:* 612-9669-4144
www.hayhouse.com.au

Published in the United Kingdom by: Hay House UK, Ltd., The Sixth Floor, Watson House, 54 Baker Street, London W1U 7BU
Phone: +44 (0)20 3927 7290 • *Fax:* +44 (0)20 3927 7291
www.hayhouse.co.uk

Published in India by: Hay House Publishers India, Muskaan Complex, Plot No. 3, B-2, Vasant Kunj, New Delhi 110 070
Phone: 91-11-4176-1620 • *Fax:* 91-11-4176-1630
www.hayhouse.co.in